UNPARALYZED

shattering
LIMITS
while finding
FREEDOM

Katie Mathews

SQUARE TREE PUBLISHING
www.SquareTreePublishing.com

For more information about bulk purchases, please contact Square Tree Publishing at info@squaretreepublishing.com.

Cover photo by Alex Shiu
Cover design by Steve Kuhn
Back Cover photo by Ruby Perez
Edited by Sheryl Martin Hash

ISBN 978-1-957293-37-0
Library of Congress Control Number: 2023924069

I am not what I ought
to be, I am not what I
want to be, I am not
what I hope to be; but
by the grace of God,
I am not what I was.

- John Newton, minister, and author
of the hymn, Amazing Grace

Dedication

This book is dedicated to my family,
who never let me give up . . . especially my mom.

TABLE OF CONTENTS

"I have told you all this so that you may have peace in me. Here on earth you will have many trials and sorrows. But take heart, because I have overcome the world." ~ John 16:33 (NLT)

Introduction

I always knew my life wouldn't be normal.

It was a feeling I'd had since early childhood, but I had no rational idea why. Oddly enough, I wasn't scared by this premonition about my future.

But I never imagined what was waiting on the path before me.

This book is about my journey—the highs, the lows, and everything in between—and how God took my shattered life and helped me find a new purpose.

I wish I could give you a detailed, firsthand account of my traumatic accident; but the truth is, I don't remember it. In some ways, I'm grateful I don't have to relive that frightful incident every day. So, much of what you'll read regarding the crash is what I've been told by those who lived it with me.

My story begins in the mountains of Jackson Hole, Wyoming. My grandparents, both teachers, moved from Iowa and settled in what was then a small town. My mom grew up there, and it was where she and my dad met and married. I arrived in 1990, and my brother, Jeff, made his debut eighteen months later. We eventually moved to Bozeman, Montana, so Mom and Dad could attend Montana State University.

One of my fondest wintertime memories of Montana is learning how to ice skate. A tennis court in the park across from our house would freeze over and turn into an ice skating rink. Our parents started Jeff and me out on the ice with a chair in front of us to keep us from falling. It didn't take long before we got enough gumption to let go of the chair, though one of our parents was always close by.

After my parents received their degrees, we moved to Colorado along with our furry family members, Blue and Abbie, beautiful chocolate labradors. I have great memories of Dad teaching us the precision and subtlety of casting a fly on the river. Mom taught us how to ski. She showed Jeff and me how to point our skis downhill to speed up or bring our ski tips together to slow down. She called these maneuvers "pizza pie" and "French fry." I preferred my skis in the French fry position to zoom down the hill as fast as I could.

Jeff and I loved exploring outside. We'd laugh as we turned over roly-polies (pill bugs), poked their bellies, and watched them frantically roll up into balls. We raced around on four-wheelers and three-wheelers. We built forts in the brush among the trees. These treasured moments along the Colorado landscape strengthened my love for nature.

Sadly, our family dynamics changed when our parents' marriage ended. Jeff stayed with Dad and Blue, and I moved with Mom and Abbie to the next town over. Divorces take an emotional toll on the entire family; dividing time with those you love is not easy. But through it all, Jeff and I knew we were blessed because we had two parents who loved us unconditionally and made every effort to ensure we knew that.

Mom eventually found a new love. When she married Brian, Jeff and I added another brother to our family. Cody lived with his mom but came to visit us every chance he could. He is fourteen months younger than Jeff; all the years I spent picking on Jeff prepared him for his own little brother! Soon, we all loved and tortured each other—as only siblings can do.

Brian's job as a corporate pilot moved us around the country a number of times. Our first adventure began when we rented an old farmhouse tucked away in the cornfields of Illinois. Although the house creeped me out, the fireflies and wide-open spaces made up for it. Three goats, a horse, and thirty chickens came with the house. My job every morning before school was to feed the chickens and collect their eggs. I always followed up this chore with a hot shower so I didn't go around smelling like the chicken coop all day!

This new town, if you could call it that, was even smaller than the one we moved from in Colorado. It featured three things: a John Deere tractor supply store, a school, and a stop sign. The school was kindergarten through grade eight, and my sixth-grade class was the largest. We had a whopping total of seventeen kids!

The next place we moved to was the complete opposite. Lincoln, Nebraska was the biggest city I'd ever lived in. My new middle school was huge. To say I was intimidated would be an understatement. But it was here that I learned something about myself: I liked being smack dab in the middle of the latest teenage drama!

Relocating was difficult for me, yet still offered many opportunities. I'm not one for stereotypes, but there was no denying that every school had cliques. Each time I started at a new school, I would sit back and watch people. I took my time reaching out to make friends. It sounds calculated, but I just knew with whom I wanted to spend my time.

While moving was challenging, it helped me to grow and understand who I am. I've been pretty competitive in most aspects of my life. Whether or not that's because I grew up with brothers is hard to say. But basketball fulfilled that competitive drive, and it was the one thing I could count on at any school I attended.

Unfortunately, our frequent moves took me farther and farther away from where my dad and Jeff lived. I saw my dad in the summertime and every other Christmas. The same was true for Mom and Jeff, and with Brian and Cody. These long separations were hard on all of us, but we were determined to make it work however we could.

Mom and Brian finally put down roots in a quaint little beach town off the Gulf Coast of Florida. I was starting the seventh grade, and once again, I took my time getting to know people. Before long, though, Kristen, Megan, and I became inseparable. We didn't live far from each other, and I am positive we wore paths between each other's houses that are still there today.

During my sophomore year of high school, we added another brother to our clan. Carson Jett definitely invigorated our family! This tiny human we all adored kept us on our toes.

After my parents' divorce, my family no longer went to the Catholic church together. My mom and I became more of the holiday churchgoers than regular attendees. But my faith and spirituality have always been strong and were never defined by just going to church. As a teenager, I saw myself as more of a spiritual person than religious. I still believed in God, Jesus, and the Holy Spirit, but my adolescent distractions overshadowed my desire to be closer to God.

Even though I felt content, the looming intuition that my life was going to change didn't sway. Whenever I saw an ambulance or visited a hospital, I got an eerie but oddly comforting feeling. I somehow knew this would become my reality one day.

I recall an instance where I had this intense feeling that my life was about to be altered forever. I was walking to one of my high school classes wearing flip-flops, a denim miniskirt, and a red Polo shirt. Tension churned in my stomach as the warm Florida sunshine beamed down on me.

I'd experienced that foreboding a few times before, but this time was different because it felt imminent. I tried to brush it off. I didn't like how it felt. I enjoyed my life, and I didn't want it to change.

But change, it did.

"Be still and know that I am God!" ~ Psalm 46:10a (NLT)

CHAPTER ONE

A SHATTERED LIFE

A few months after my sixteenth birthday, on May 6, 2006, life as I knew it came to a screeching halt.

It started out much like any other weekend. Our high school basketball season had ended, so I played AAU (Amateur Athletic Union) basketball in the offseason. One of my best friends, Chelsea, was also on the team and had recently gotten her driver's license. So, we would have a blast driving to the games together—talking, singing, dancing along to the music, and enjoying our newfound freedom.

I received the All-Tournament player award at the tournament we played in that weekend. It is given to the person who plays an integral role in helping her team succeed. I had been striving for this achievement ever since I started playing club (travel) basketball. Needless to say, I was pretty happy after the tournament.

Chelsea and I felt like celebrating, so we decided to go to a friend's party at his ranch. This wasn't the kind of party my mom would allow me to attend; so instead, I got her permission to spend the night at Chelsea's house, which was my alibi.

Around 10:45 p.m., we headed to our friend's ranch—our minds were on the party and not much else. We giggled about who would be there and all the usual high school gossip. In the midst of our bantering, we realized we didn't know how to get to the ranch. I called a friend to give us directions.

We were about to pass our exit, still in the far-left lane. Chelsea swung the steering wheel to the right. As soon as the wheels crossed into the next lane, I felt the vehicle begin to lean.

Chelsea and I exchanged glances of terror, knowing something horrible was about to happen.

In sheer panic, she jerked the steering wheel hard in the opposite direction. Instantly, we began barrel rolling to the left, flipping four times before the SUV landed upright in the median.

Off-duty paramedics were driving by and witnessed everything. They immediately rushed to our aid.

"I don't think she's breathing!" Chelsea shouted frantically, gesturing to me.

My body was slumped over in the passenger seat, unresponsive, with only my seatbelt keeping me upright. A female paramedic ran over to my side of the car.

"Is she seven?" her coworker asked as he assessed Chelsea. (Signal seven is code for a deceased person).

"She has a pulse!" the female paramedic yelled back in relief. She began to pull my limp body from the wreckage. A tube was immediately placed into my airway so I could get oxygen. The paramedics carefully placed me into one of the two helicopters that had arrived to take Chelsea and me to the nearest trauma center.

Jon, the paramedic who was first on the scene, told me sometime later that he didn't think I was alive when he helped lift me into the helicopter.

"Still, I felt compelled to call the local Christian radio station right after the helicopter took off," he told me. "I asked the listeners to pray for you and Chelsea."

Other emergency medical personnel were trying to keep Chelsea calm as they stabilized her neck and assessed her injuries. The steering wheel had embedded itself into her femur, requiring the Jaws of Life tool to pry her from the car. She was in extreme pain and terrified, not knowing if she'd ever see me again.

Mom and Brian heard the news when a police officer knocked on their door in the middle of the night.

“Sir, your daughter has been in a car crash and is being airlifted to Saint Petersburg Trauma Center,” the policeman told my stepdad.

Fear mixed with adrenaline shot through my mom when she overheard the conversation. She had to see me NOW. She immediately ran to collect my nine-month-old baby brother from his crib. The policeman asked Brian to step out onto the front porch. The officer fidgeted with his hands as he searched for the right words.

“You need to prepare your wife, sir, on the drive to the hospital,” he told Brian solemnly. “There is a good chance your daughter won’t make it through the night.”

My mom and Carson were already buckled in when Brian sprinted to the car. He drove off with the front door still open and the lights on in the house. About five minutes later, they passed the vehicle Chelsea and I had been in—a heap of twisted metal and scattered belongings.

With a lump in her throat and the image of the wreckage burned into her memory, my mom frantically tried to reach someone in the emergency room. Her call was transferred to the hospital chaplain, who told her I was in stable condition and to focus on getting to the hospital safely.

To dig deeper into this chapter, turn to page 166 for Discussion Questions.

"The Lord is close to the brokenhearted and saves those who are crushed in spirit." ~ Psalm 34:18 (NIV)

CHAPTER TWO

A GRIM PROGNOSIS

Doctors and surgeons at the trauma center worked tirelessly to keep me alive. My mom was nearly hysterical trying to find out the condition of her sixteen-year-old baby girl.

"Please, please let me go back to see her!" she pleaded desperately with the nurses.

"Ma'am, your daughter is not in stable condition, and no one is permitted to see her at this time," a nurse gently told her. My mom's heart sank as the words "not stable" registered deep in her soul. She slumped into a nearby chair as an unexplainable ache consumed her body.

All she could do was wait.

She and Brian were later taken to a private room where they met with the trauma surgeon and the chaplain. The doctor's assessment was vastly different from what the chaplain had led them to believe. The surgeon bluntly rattled off the facts as if he were reading from a spreadsheet.

"Your daughter's most significant injuries right now are a broken neck and compromised lungs, which are in critical condition. We aren't concerned about her other injuries because, at this point, we are just trying to keep her alive."

My stepdad glared at the chaplain. "Why did you lie to us?" he demanded.

"If I had recounted exactly what was going on with your daughter, there was a good chance your emotions may have overwhelmed you," the chaplain explained. "I didn't want panic to set in, so I told you she was stable to get you to the hospital safely."

My dad soon arrived from California and was updated on my condition.

A long day and a half later, I was stable enough to proceed with neck surgery. Two cervical vertebrae along the base of my neck were shattered, so the neurosurgeon restructured my spine using titanium. He told my family the surgery went better than expected, and I should no longer have problems with the stability of my neck in that area.

His voice grew grave as he explained that my spinal cord was the only thing he couldn't fix.

"The shards of bone from the demolished vertebrae punctured her spinal cord in several areas along the base of her neck, resulting in a C 6/7 spinal cord injury," he explained. "With her level of injury, she will be classified as a quadriplegic."

My family was devastated. It meant I would no longer have control over any body parts below my chest, including my hands and fingers, and minimal use of my arms.

My damaged lungs were also a part of this paralysis; they no longer had the ability to function on their own. I was now dependent on machines to breathe for me. The trauma surgeon came into my hospital room every day to clear my lungs, a meticulous and time-consuming effort. Amidst all the other battles my body was facing, my lungs staying clean was imperative if I was going to have any quality of life again—especially living as a quadriplegic.

I was placed in a medically-induced coma so my body could rest and try to heal. After two weeks, they began to slowly bring me out of the coma. The neurosurgeon was then able to evaluate how my brain was affected by the crash.

"There are three different ways in which Katie's brain was injured," he told my family.

“She sustained a frontal contusion when her head struck an object with blunt force. Signs of sheering are prevalent, which occur when the brain is thrashed around inside the skull. I also found signs of an anoxic brain injury, which means her brain didn’t receive oxygen for a period of time.”

No oxygen to the brain often renders a person brain-dead within a short period of time. However, the paramedic had quickly intubated me at the crash site so oxygen could continue flowing to my brain. I will always be grateful for his fast response.

A few weeks after I was brought out of the coma, I still wasn’t showing any signs of improvement. My brain injuries became the point of concern. I lay in my hospital bed, unresponsive, with machines and IVs quite literally keeping me alive. The trauma surgeon came in to speak to my mother.

“What do you and your family want for Katie?” he asked tersely.

“Well, once she is cleared from the ICU, we are looking into brain and spinal cord injury rehab hospitals where we can take her,” my mother responded.

“If, or when, Katie comes out of the coma she’s lapsed into, there is a good chance she will be in a vegetative state for the rest of her life," the surgeon replied. "I recommend you talk with your family about her well-being and consider taking her off life support."

My mother was stunned.

"Is she brain-dead?"

"Well . . . no," the doctor responded hesitantly.

"Okay, then. You keep doing everything you can to keep my daughter alive," she replied, glaring daggers at him.

My loved ones didn't accept the surgeon's grim prognosis about my future. My dad would fly to Florida as often as possible and say the rosary by my hospital bed each night. We all believed that with God, all things are possible—even in our darkest hour.

My Aunt Vicki (who is actually my mom's cousin) came from Arkansas to stay with me one night at the hospital. She ordered my mom and Brian to go out for dinner, and she wouldn't take no for an answer. She knew they badly needed a break.

No sooner did they leave than my five-foot, ball-of-fire aunt climbed onto my bed and placed her head close to mine. She told my seemingly lifeless body that we were going to do something to surprise my mom.

"I know you're in there, Katie. I know you can hear me. Will you do something that would mean the world to everyone who loves you? Will you say 'mom'?"

Vicki kept this going for I don't know how long until my lips mouthed the word "mom." My aunt was thrilled. She kept coaching me until my mom and Brian returned from dinner.

"We have a surprise for you," Vicki told them excitedly.

She asked me to say the word again. Tears of joy streamed down my mother's cheeks as my lips formed her name. While I still had a long way to go, I wasn't in a vegetative state at all.

My mom rarely left my bedside, and her positive energy flowed to me. She knew her baby girl was still somewhere within that fractured body, so she would play the music I loved and speak encouraging words over me. She instituted a rule for my friends who wanted to visit: only good energy was allowed.

If anyone needed to cry after seeing their once vibrant friend now lying unrecognizable in a hospital bed, she asked them to quietly step out of my room. My two best friends, Kristen and Megan, and my boyfriend came to see me almost every day after school. Kristen and Megan would sit next to my bed and fill me in on all of the high school gossip—just like we'd always done. I was so glad some things didn't change just because I was lying unresponsive in a hospital bed.

Chelsea was healing from a broken femur and had to undergo surgery to remove muscles in her calf where infection had spread. Thankfully, she was able to return home after a few weeks.

So many individuals reached out to help my family during this time. One of their biggest blessings was being able to stay at the Ronald McDonald House while I was in the ICU. Thoughtful men and women in our community joined together to meet any need we had. Not to mention the countless family, friends, and people I didn't even know who were praying for me.

My stepdad worked for an evangelist whose church was not far from the hospital. Members of her church—whom I had never met—brought food to my family, stood beside my bed, and prayed with them. I believe all these caring souls' prayers, love, support, and positive energy, in collaboration with the power of the Holy Spirit, kept my heart beating.

After five long weeks in the ICU, I was ready to take the next step on my road to recovery. Surgeons, doctors, and the care team at the St. Petersburg ICU had done everything they could to bring my once hopeless body back to life. But there was still so much left to do.

To dig deeper into this chapter, turn to page 167 for Discussion Questions.

"For I know the plans I have for you," declares the Lord, "plans to prosper you and not to harm you, plans to give you hope and a future."
~ Jeremiah 29:11 (NIV)

CHAPTER THREE

THE MISSING YEARS

Several family members started researching the best brain and spinal cord injury rehab centers around the country. But there was one caveat: the rehab center needed to accept me.

Representatives from several centers came to assess whether their services would be a good match for my needs. I was accepted into two of the best facilities in the country. While the rehab center in Atlanta was much closer to home—which meant an easier transition for my family—the Craig Rehabilitation Center in Denver, Colorado, was determined to be a better fit. A few days later, I was medically airlifted to the center.

For the next several months, my mom and Brian put their lives on hold. My mom took leave from work and moved with my stepdad and baby brother from Florida to Colorado. An apartment not far from the rehab hospital became their temporary home; now they could be by my side through everything. My crash didn't just affect me—it also substantially impacted the lives of my loved ones.

Shortly after I arrived at the rehab center, I started to regress and slipped into an unresponsive state. I was taken to the Swedish Hospital, which adjoined the rehab center through what seemed to be never-ending hallways. I made that trek for tests and scans more times than I can count.

Even though I was unresponsive, I was still awake. I dreaded those tests because of the nausea that ensued from lying on my back, looking up at the ceiling, not knowing which way I would be turned next. On the other hand, these trips to the Swedish Hospital pretty much secured my being in bed all day—which was all I wanted to do anyway.

I had a large lump in the back of my neck, which doctors determined was spinal cord fluid. Initially, they weren't concerned because this fluid was supposed to be absorbed by my body. That didn't happen. After conducting a brain scan, they discovered that the spinal fluid traveled into my head, putting pressure on my brain and causing me to go into a stupor. I immediately had emergency surgery to place a ventriculoperitoneal (VP) shunt into my skull. this would drain the extra fluid and relieve the pressure on my brain.

Rejoining my life cognitively was terrifying and disorienting for me. My traumatic brain injury caused severe, short-term memory loss. In the early stages, it was rare for me to remember anything from one day to the next. The world in which I now lived seemed to be set on repeat. The previous three years of my life had also been erased from my recollection.

Though I had just celebrated my sixteenth birthday a few months before the crash, my brain insisted I was thirteen. My brother Carson was born during those three missing years.

"Who is this tiny human crawling around my room?" I would ask my mom over and over.

Multiple times a day, I questioned why I couldn't move, forgetting the answer I was given only moments before. Since I didn't remember the accident, I didn't understand why I couldn't control my body below chest level. I finally decided the culprits were all the IVs connected to me and the numerous medications the staff continually gave me. I didn't believe the doctors were helping me, but rather they were causing me to be trapped inside my own body.

I felt isolated because no one understood what I believed to be true. I had no idea how I ended up in this so-called rehab hospital. The last thing I remembered was being a thirteen-year-old girl with a functioning body. Now, here I was in bed with a broken body, and my family and doctors were trying to convince me I was sixteen.

Something inside kept telling me not to believe their falsehoods. Even though these people looked and sounded like my family, my delusional brain convinced me my real family wouldn't feed me lies about a reality I didn't understand existed. I honestly believed I was in a different universe, some form of hell, so they couldn't be my real family. Even so, I was grateful they were with me. They were the only ones I could really count on, and their love was my only source of comfort.

Prickling pain was my constant companion. The only areas I could actually feel were from my arms up, but I had a constant burning sensation throughout my body. The closest comparison is the pins-and-needles feeling you get when your foot falls asleep. Only for me, this intense sensation never went away.

I also suffered recurring migraines, where the least bit of light or sound made me want to shrivel up in pain or vomit. Sitting upright was another challenge. I had been lying horizontally in a hospital bed for over a month. Being in the seated position made my head feel like it was being squeezed so tightly it would burst. This feeling left me dizzy, nauseous, and like I was going to pass out.

So most of the time, when I was rolling around the halls, I would recline my power wheelchair seat as far back as I could and still manage to drive. For the first few months at Craig, just sitting in my chair took all the stamina I had, so therapy on top of it seemed like torture. Nonetheless, therapy was required, no matter how much I protested.

One of the more unpleasant consequences of my condition was phlegm accumulating in my throat. Nurses would place a suction tube into my tracheotomy to suck it out. I hated this! Eventually, the nurses trained my family how to do this.

My dad looked at Jeff, who was fourteen at the time, and said, "You should probably learn how to do this too," and handed him the suction device.

My brother and I have always been close, but all the times I tortured him started running through my head. So I was terrified when my dad encouraged Jeff to try. This is perfect payback, I thought as I glared at my dad.

With the nurse instructing him, Jeff slowly took the suction tube and gently placed it into the hole in my neck. He pulled it back out with just as much care. Later, he confided how nervous he had been.

"I was just as scared as you were," he assured me. It seems like a strange thing to bond over, but since that moment, we have been closer than ever.

One of the reasons we chose Craig for my rehab was their process for weaning me off my tracheotomy—and I was all for it. Each day, the nurses would increase the amount of time I could stay off my tracheotomy and breathe independently. It was definitely a process, and my body took a while to adjust into a new rhythm. But I'm so grateful it did!

Regaining my ability to eat wasn't that big of a deal for me. I had been receiving nutrients from a feeding tube for over a month. My extreme nausea caused me to lose a lot of weight; and let's face it, hospital food isn't the most delicious!

It's a bit ironic that the last thing I wanted to do was eat—yet people could bribe me with certain foods, especially sweets. If you wanted me to sit up for an extra minute or two, just motivate me with chocolate! My family tempted me with irresistible root beer floats at a nearby ice cream shop. Even though this outing meant I would be in an upright position for longer than usual, I would suck up the pain and roll on, knowing my reward awaited me.

Then there were my aunt and uncle, who didn't live too far from the hospital. Their bribe of choice was bringing me Outback steaks. Those were some of the rare times I would actually eat a full meal.

But my dad's visits were the most entertaining for me at mealtime. We would go to the cafeteria in the Swedish Hospital—for some reason, their food was just better. While I needed to take breaks occasionally as we rolled through the maze of hallways, I knew it was going to be worth it. I would completely gross out my dad by ordering the California rolls. Watching him cringe as he put the cooked crab sushi roll in my mouth was hilarious!

My mom did her best to stimulate my mind by decorating my room at Craig with pictures, poster boards, and anything that might make me smile. She even put pictures on the ceiling, so I was surrounded by memories of laughter and love as I lay on my back. I would study those photos, and occasionally people and events came back to life for me. I desperately wanted to be back in that reality again.

Slipping into depression was an easy transition for me. The only place I wanted to be was in bed because I was not expected to do anything. I didn't have to sit up, I didn't have to eat, I didn't have to talk. I didn't have to do much that related to being a human being. For that very reason, I'm pretty sure my days spent in bed were few and far between.

On numerous occasions, I would lie in my hospital bed and stare at the second hand ticking away on the clock hanging across from me. I would fixate on that second hand, waiting for it to either skip or stop. I was desperate for proof that this impossible world I was now living in wasn't my new reality. Some mornings, I would lie with my eyes closed and pray: Please let the nurses and my family have empathy and let me stay in bed today. Most of the time, however, I was unsuccessful.

One of my most motivational moments involved my love for country music. My mom heard that country music singer Rodney Atkins and his band were coming to Craig to perform for us. I wasn't feeling the best after therapy that day, but that was nothing new. My headaches had prevented me from listening to music for a long time, and I missed it. But I wasn't about to let this opportunity to enjoy music again pass me by.

I parked my wheelchair among all the others in the large therapy room where Rodney and his band were setting up. Before long, I started to feel nauseous, and I was almost certain a headache was brewing. I leaned my chair back, determined that my body would not rob me of this experience. As soon as the music started, my ears perked up, and I was no longer trapped in discomfort. Immediately, I began swaying along to the music.

One song in particular grabbed hold of me. The chorus to "If You're Going Through Hell" spoke to my heart as Rodney sang.[1] I had heard this song before, but at that moment, it felt as if its motivating lyrics were written just for me. I began humming along, reassuring myself that I would keep going within the hell I felt like I was in.

As my mom and I rolled back to my room, we danced and sang along to the upbeat rhythm. Lying in bed that night, I was so happy I hadn't given in to my pain and left the concert. I couldn't imagine missing out on that pivotal moment that gave me a much-needed boost of determination. I drifted off to sleep with a new sense of hope.

1Rodney Atkins, 2006. "If You're Going Through Hell (Before the Devil Even Knows)." Track 10 on "If You're Going Through Hell." Curb Records, compact disc.

My stamina for sitting up improved after a few months of relentless pestering to get me into my chair every day. This meant I could finally enjoy spending time outside with my family and other visitors. I especially looked forward to spending time at my aunt and uncle's home. They had no idea how much those precious outings meant to me. It was a breath of fresh air to spend time with them and my cousins after staring at the walls of the hospital for so long.

Another favorite outing was going to the mall, something I had enjoyed since my early teens. And the mall near the rehab didn't disappoint. It contained a small Godiva chocolate store. Since anything chocolate is my weakness, I invariably made a point to visit this store, no matter what.

I was also overjoyed I had built up enough endurance to celebrate Carson's first birthday. We took him to the Denver aquarium. Watching my little brother's face light up meant the world to me. While I absolutely loathed rehab, it allowed me to be an active part in this celebration and many more in Denver.

I had made a lot of progress, but I still had times of intense pain, so most of my outings were short. Still, I cherished each one. Many of our friends and family went out of their way to care for us and love on us. From visiting us in Colorado, helping with tasks back home, or making a phone call and lifting us up in prayer, it was their compassion that helped us keep going.

When my dad visited, we would stroll to the Catholic church nearby and attend Sunday mass. But before we set out, Dad and I would come up with a short list of things I would try to find on our way—such as a person wearing a hat or someone walking a dog. This was very difficult for me at first, but the more I practiced, the more I could remember without him giving me tons of hints.

One day as we got into the elevator at rehab, my dad asked me what floor we were going to as he gestured at all the buttons. I began to panic as I stared at the numbered buttons that leered back at me.

"One…?" I asked hesitantly.

He nodded and said, "Okay, now push it."

I looked at him in disbelief. I awkwardly maneuvered my wheelchair closer to the buttons. When I finally got to the right place, I reached out and pushed the number. Lo and behold, we started moving! I was elated!

I turned to my dad with the goofiest of smiles, which grew even bigger when I saw him smiling too. I had done something for myself! I had taken another step on my journey to independence.

Not long after that, I was rolling back to my room solo after therapy. Usually, my mom was with me, but this day was different. I looked out the windows as I passed by and longed to be in the garden: breathing in fresh air, listening to the chirping birds, smelling the flowers, and soaking in the sunshine. Suddenly, I noticed the elevators and remembered that day with my dad. I knew I could do it again. Soon, I was reclining in my wheelchair, relaxing in the warmth of the sun, happy to be outside.

This was my favorite spot at the rehab center—sitting among the trees and flowers. Although I guess technically it wasn't a garden, it was a garden oasis to me. I must have lost track of time, because the next thing I knew, my mom was rushing toward me.

"Where have you been?! Your therapist said you went straight back to your room after therapy. But I went to your room, and you weren't there! We've been looking everywhere for you!"

As her panicked voice turned into relief, I explained that I wanted to be in the sunshine. She smiled as she exhaled and wrapped her arms around me.

"Well, I guess I can't ground you," she joked. We both laughed.

"Next time, please just let someone know where you are going," she added softly as we embraced again. We both knew this was a big step for me. I had wanted something, and instead of waiting for someone else to do it for me, I took the initiative and did it myself.

Craig's chapel was located next to my room, and I don't believe that was a coincidence. I would go in there on my own or with my family and quietly ask God why this was happening to me. Even though I never got a clear response, I felt calmer whenever I was in there.

It was strange, because I was angry with God for allowing me to be in this situation. I also was still confused whether this was reality at all; yet I felt at peace. These emotions overwhelmed me, and I had a hard time wrapping my brain around them. All I knew was I needed to go home.

Mom hung a calendar in my room and circled and starred the day in October we would head home. We counted down the days by drawing a big X through each date that passed. I got excited as I watched my mom put an X through another number. I wanted to go home so badly. I craved familiarity, and for some reason, I thought things would return to normal once I moved back home.

At least that's what I desperately hoped.

To dig deeper into this chapter, turn to page 169 for Discussion Questions.

"Finally, brothers and sisters, whatever is true, whatever is noble, whatever is right, whatever is pure, whatever is lovely, whatever is admirable—if anything is excellent or praiseworthy—think about such things." ~ Philippians 4:8 (NIV)

CHAPTER FOUR

A NEW NORMAL

When I finally got home, it wasn't at all what I expected.

My family had moved into a new house several months before my crash—which meant I had no recollection of ever living there. After five months in the hospital and rehab, I had envisioned things would start making sense once I was back in familiar surroundings. I even thought my body would finally have a chance to return to normal too.

But I didn't recognize this house. It didn't offer me the comfort and security I craved. And my body still didn't work. I was more frustrated than ever.

Realizing this, my mom and Brian took me on a short drive to the house where we used to live. As we passed by, I breathed a sigh of relief. This house held so many good memories for me. And while it was now a part of my past, the fact it was real helped me be okay with moving forward.

In a strange way, just seeing that house was like a stamp of approval. It assured me that this was indeed my reality, not the hell I had convinced myself of at Craig. It also forced me to come to terms with my brokenness . . . I could no longer believe it wasn't real.

Uselessness and even hopelessness crushed me as I began living my new normal. I was totally dependent on another person in every aspect of my life—from simplicities like opening a door to something as personal as going to the bathroom. For example, what used to be a semi- quick, independent morning routine had turned into a four-hour endeavor with my caregiver.

I constantly needed to interrupt someone else to help me do something I used to accomplish with ease. Even though I was blessed with a devoted support system of family and friends, I knew my continual neediness was a burden on those I loved.

I*t would be better for everyone if I weren't living anymore,* I often thought. I honestly didn't want to live this life I was now facing. I was angry at my situation and the position I put my friends and family in. I felt sorry for myself. And I was mad at an all-powerful God for not stepping in to prevent my circumstances.

I began to spiral down the defeated and lonely slide of self-pity. I couldn't see anything ahead of me because my focus was behind me. I was filled with agonizing regret over the decisions I desperately wished I could undo. Though my mind was in a dark place, it was the only place that felt familiar in a world that had become foreign to me.

Not only was I trying to cope with my defective body, I was also trying to make sense of a brain that no longer worked as well. Every time I considered what my future could hold, it was as if I were looking into a mirror that just reflected my broken body and my clouded mind.

I struggled to accept that the future I had always wanted and planned for was no longer attainable. *Good and gracious God, why would You want me to be broken, with no worthwhile future in sight?*

Despite these bleak thoughts, I was still appreciative for my lifeline of friends and family. My friends, including Megan and Kristen, visited countless times trying to jog my memory about events from those missing three years. They told stories of our past shenanigans, and sometimes those memories would return to me. When that happened, it spurred them to keep at it.

Family and members of our community went out of their way to make me feel welcomed and as comfortable as possible. Brian and some family friends built a large ramp so

I could bypass the stairs going into our house. My stepdad also oversaw the remodel of my bathroom to make sure it was adapted to my needs.

My dad and Jeff moved out of their condo, which had many stairs, and into a house that didn't. Dad built ramps for the stairs that were there, so I could be a part of life in California too. Our community put together fundraisers for Chelsea and me to help with our medical costs. I don't think I fully realized how much my injury impacted so many other people around me.

One of my family's most important needs was a wheelchair-accessible van. My 400-pound power wheelchair wouldn't fit in our family car, so we needed a specialty van with a ramp. They came with a hefty price tag, so we made do with what we had.

Whenever I went out, my power wheelchair stayed at home, and Mom would lift me into her car. During these outings, I was confined to my manual wheelchair, which was much easier to travel with but also very limiting. My right arm was in a constant contraction at the elbow from my injury, which made it difficult to maneuver a manual wheelchair. The worst part was this chair once again made me reliant on someone else.

We had a family friend who continually asked Brian what we needed and if she could help in any way. My stepdad didn't want to impose such a big expense on anyone, so he didn't mention the van. She wasn't the type to sit idly by, so she asked around and discovered our need. She and her church blessed us beyond measure by gifting us a wheelchair-accessible van.

It seemed I had everything I needed: a loving support system, a home and vehicle that were fitted to my needs, and compassionate caregivers who came every morning to help me get ready to start my day. Yet, I couldn't shake the thoughts that filled my head. I'll never be as fun or as valuable as I once was.

These lies insisted my real life was in the past. The monotony of my life now was just going through the motions as other people literally did everything for me. I was stuck in my own misery. It was as if a dark, gray veil covered my eyes, allowing me to only see the brokenness in my life.

My mom knew being around my friends again and getting back into a familiar routine would be good for me. She enrolled me back in high school halfway through my junior year. My high school was reluctant because they had never accommodated someone with my needs before. They offered to send a tutor to our house so I could finish high school at home.

I have always been a social butterfly, and my mom knew that being away from my friends and missing out on high school experiences wouldn't be good for me. She met with school officials numerous times to figure out the best ways for them to accommodate me. My high school agreed to do whatever they could to have me back.

Mom was right. Returning to high school was one of the best, yet most challenging, things I could've done at that point in my life. My chronic fatigue and the length of time it took for someone to help me get ready meant I went to school only half days. On my first day back, my mom and I waited for the bus at the end of our driveway. I was overjoyed to see a full-sized bus with a wheelchair lift. I know it may be vain, but I didn't want to make my entrance back into high school by riding the short (handicapped) bus.

As we pulled up to campus, a lady standing by the flag poles was waiting for me. She introduced herself as Mrs. Thompson.

"Hi, Katie, we're so glad to have you back! You can call me Mary if you like. I've been hired to help you with anything you need," she said, smiling.

I immediately liked her personality and could sense we'd have a good connection. She looked much younger than any of the teachers I was used to seeing. We made our way to a smaller building where a special desk—a table with a half circle cut out for my wheelchair—had been set up for me.

This is where I would complete my work and where Mary and I would spend our time between classes. Because I no longer had control over my fingers, she was my scribe, amongst all the other things she helped me with. We needed a place where I could dictate my papers to her without disrupting the rest of the class.

Before long, I realized school no longer came as easily as it once had. I used to be in mostly honors classes, and remembering things came naturally to me. Now, remembering what I had for breakfast was a feat. Not only was my schoolwork a challenge, but how others viewed me had also changed. My friends still saw me as Katie, but I could see the stares from other students as I rolled around campus. It was oh-so evident that I was different.

As I was crying to my mom one night about my unfair situation, she looked at me with stern but loving eyes and said something that ultimately became my turning point.

"You have two choices in life, Katie. You can either be miserable, dwelling on the past with demoralizing regret about what could have been; or you can give thanks for the life you still have and move forward. While your old way of life may have died in that car crash, you didn't. You are still very much alive to create a new future for yourself."

Her message was hard to hear and even harder to accept. But I got it. If I ever wanted to be happy again, I had to let go of my old life and the things I once wanted to accomplish.

So, I decided I didn't want to be miserable anymore. Monitoring my thoughts was exhausting and tedious, but looking back, it was the best decision I could have made. Whenever I started to think, poor me, I replaced it with a more uplifting thought. For instance, when I put on the bulky, ugly fork or spoon adaption that fastened the utensil to my hand, I would think, *Ugh, why can't I just go back to picking up a fork or spoon like I used to? This is so embarrassing.*

But I'd quickly change that to, *Yes, but I am glad to have these utensils so I can feed myself!*

After practicing this new point of view for a while, good thoughts started to outweigh the bad. Eventually, the negative thoughts just disappeared.

Once I decided to think positively, my world began to look brighter. My life wasn't as bad as I imagined. The anger, frustration, and discouragement I had been holding onto blinded me from all the good still around me.

Though I was discovering a new appreciation for my life, students' lingering stares still made me feel self-conscious. I broke down once again as I explained to my mom how they reminded me that I was different from everyone else.

She opened my mind with one question: "What would you think if you saw someone rolling past you at school in a wheelchair?"

Surprisingly, it didn't take long for me to blurt out an answer. "I'd most likely be curious about why they were in that position."

She smiled as she said, "Well, that may be what they are wondering too."

That night, I concluded those looks might not be disapproval—as I had imagined—but were prompted by curiosity and not knowing how to approach me. From then on, I rolled up to whomever I saw gazing in my direction and started talking. Once the ice was broken, their focus shifted from the chair to me. I was then seen as Katie, a girl who just happened to be sitting in a wheelchair.

I really began to enjoy school again and made some cherished lifelong memories. One of my fondest was during my senior year when my class voted me onto the Homecoming Court. The night the Homecoming King and Queen were announced was a beautiful Florida night. At halftime of the varsity football game, we were driven onto the field, each couple sitting in cool-looking old cars.

Mike, a good friend of mine and also a member of the Homecoming Court, picked me up and put me in the front seat of one of the cars. I felt so special as I waved at the fans in the stands cheering and waving back. Mike drove my wheelchair onto the field, then came to get me out of the car to set me in it. He stood next to me as the proceedings got underway. When Mike's name was announced as Homecoming King, I was cheering so loudly with the crowd I barely heard them name the Homecoming Queen.

When I realized my name was called, I froze.

Just a year earlier, I was timidly making my way back to school on a wheelchair bus. I was scared and intimidated, unsure if I wanted to be there. I had convinced myself people were staring at me because I was different; and let's face it, being different in high school rarely feels like a good thing.

Now, here I was, receiving the biggest honor anyone could get as a high school student—my peers voting me as Homecoming Queen.

A day I once imagined would never come had finally arrived. I was graduating high school with my classmates. It took hard work and discipline to make that day a reality. I was touched and honored when asked to deliver the final speech, sending my fellow classmates out into the world and closing the chapter on our high school years.

Later, the school principal approached my mom and me and told us they had initially been leery of having me on campus.

"We really didn't know if we were prepared to accommodate Katie's needs. But it worked so well, we have enrolled another girl in a wheelchair for the upcoming school year," she said. "Mrs. Miller, thank you for pushing us to have Katie come back."

I had come a long way since my prognosis nearly two years earlier when I was lying in a hospital bed, unresponsive. I was most definitely not living in a vegetative state, despite my doctor's warning. I am grateful God had a different plan for my life.

Nevertheless, I remained apprehensive about speaking to God. Even though my mindset had shifted and I was making peace with my new life, I periodically had breakdowns, asking *Why me?* amid sobs. If it were up to me, I would not be confined to a wheelchair, needing assistance in every aspect of my daily life. I still didn't see any good that could come from my broken body and the dependency it forced me to have on others.

To dig deeper into this chapter, turn to page 170 for Discussion Questions.

"Don't worry about anything; instead, pray about everything. Tell God what you need, and thank Him for all He has done. Then you will experience God's peace, which exceeds anything we can understand. His peace will guard your hearts and minds as you live in Christ Jesus."
~ Philippians 4:6-7 (NLT)

CHAPTER FIVE

WHAT'S NEXT?

Have you ever watched the classic 1993 movie, *Groundhog Day?* It's the story of a television weatherman who becomes trapped in a time loop, reliving the same day over and over.

That was my life once school no longer filled my days. Time seemed to slow to a turtle's pace as one uneventful day dragged into the next. Each morning was the same: waking up to the smell of coffee brewing, hearing my mother trying to corral my two-year-old brother into sitting still to eat his breakfast, and her coming in to give me a hug before she left for work.

Amid all the morning commotion, my caregiver would arrive. I relied on her capable hands for everything that involved getting ready for the day. I used to spend about an hour grooming myself for the day ahead; after my paralysis, that time more than quadrupled—and I could barely contribute in any way.

Even so, I was grateful for a young caregiver who didn't make me feel like I was a chore.

We talked and laughed throughout the morning routine. Because we spent so much time together, we built a strong bond, growing more of a friendship than a typical caregiver-patient relationship.

Once we jumped through all the hoops on the checklist of "getting Katie up and ready," we made our way to the living room. As I parallel parked myself next to the couch, she retrieved the lunch Mom had left me in the refrigerator. After placing a tray on my lap for my computer and lunch, my caregiver would leave me with a great big hug. I spent the majority of my day there until my family returned home.

I eagerly scrolled through social media to see what was happening in my friends' lives. But as I stared at that computer screen, reading post after post about them going off to college, I became extremely discouraged and a little angry.

That should be me! That should be my life! I should be making arrangements to move into a new dorm room and experience this season of life with old friends and new ones.

Everything I had planned for my life was being played out on the computer screen in front of me. I felt lost, hopeless, and to be honest, worthless. I couldn't even get myself into or out of bed without depending on another person.

My loved ones did their best to lift my spirits, but they didn't fully comprehend the devil's lies and schemes swirling inside my head.

You'll never amount to anything! You can't be a productive part of society or even help yourself, for that matter.

It felt as if all the doors I had once seen open for me were being slammed shut in my face. The depression that once blinded me from seeing anything good crept back into my life.

I tried to keep a smile on my face, but the debilitating emotions were obvious to those closest to me. As I was crying to my mom one evening, all those feelings came flooding out.

"I don't see any worthwhile future for myself. I need assistance to do everything! I feel like a speed bump in everyone's day with my constant interruptions for help. Mom, I honestly think it would have been better for everyone if I had died in that car crash. And if I'm truly honest, I don't want to live anymore."

I can't imagine how hard it was for my mom to hear those words. Yet, somehow she already knew I was battling demons.

She looked at me as if her heart would break.

"Katie, I was so worried you were having these feelings again."

She leaned in and embraced me as we both cried for what seemed like hours. When we finished hugging, she asked, "Sweetie, would it be okay if we prayed?"

I sighed hesitantly as I remembered the last time I had prayed. It was in the chapel at the rehab hospital in Colorado, pleading with God for an answer as to why He let this happen to me. I had been desperate for Him to tell me this was just a dream, not my reality. However, I never got that response. I felt betrayed by an all-powerful God.

But as I stared into my mother's red-rimmed eyes, I knew I was at rock bottom. I gave her a small nod.

She clasped her warm hands around mine, and we bowed our heads as she began to speak softly through her tears. Her first words were of gratitude. That was not what I expected. When I thought of my brokenness, I couldn't see any reason to be thankful.

"Dear God, thank you for allowing my daughter to still have breath in her lungs and a future before her." Mom paused and took a few calming breaths. "While the future we once planned for is no longer in sight, please show us in our hearts the future *You* have planned for Katie. Amen."

It was a simple prayer, but it was vulnerable and raw. Mom lifted me out of my wheelchair and helped me to bed, then kissed my forehead before turning to leave. As she closed the door, I was overcome with gratefulness for her. It was almost as if light shone through that dark, gray veil the enemy had placed over my eyes. It was a good feeling.

In the days that followed, I tried to find gratitude once more. But frankly, it seemed like a chore because I was already exhausted. I wasn't sure how to begin feeling glad again; all I knew was I didn't have a lot of precious energy to spare.

I mentioned this dilemma to my mom. She clasped my limp hand and said she had an idea. "I want you to find three things you are truly grateful for each day," she said.

That seemed like such an enormous undertaking because my thoughts were still focused on, *Why me?* My mom could tell I was overwhelmed by her suggestion.

"Don't worry, sweetie, we will look together to find the first ray of gratitude in the morning," she assured me.

Once again, light started to shine through that dark gray veil of negativity. I was empowered knowing that she was with me in this fight.

After that, I began to consciously seek out things I felt were worthy of my gratitude. I knew it would use my fleeting energy, but I longed to enjoy positivity in my life again.

The more I practiced this attitude, the less time I spent wallowing in self-pity. I realized I had more power over my mindset than I knew. Whether I indulged in the light of positivity or the slugfest of negativity, it set the tone for my day. I promised myself that even on the dark days, I would find at least three beacons of light for which to be grateful.

Quite honestly, I was a little taken aback by the simplicity of the things for which I was genuinely thankful:

- the warm, Florida sun shining on my face
- the ability to feed myself (even if it was with an embarrassingly ugly fork)
- the love and support I received from my family and friends

These were things I'd had all along; I just didn't have eyes willing to see them. But oh, how liberating it was when I shifted my focus and appreciated the life I am so blessed to have.

I was reminded of the advice Glinda the Good Witch gave Dorothy in *The Wizard of Oz*: "You always had the power, my dear, you just had to learn it for yourself."

To dig deeper into this chapter, turn to page 172 for Discussion Questions.

"My thoughts are nothing like your thoughts," says the Lord. "And My ways are far beyond anything you could imagine. For just as the heavens are higher than the earth, so My ways are higher than your ways and My thoughts higher than your thoughts."
~ Isaiah 55:8-9 (NLT)

CHAPTER SIX

GOD SENDS A UNICORN

While I may have been hesitant to talk to God, He didn't hesitate to show His continual love and care for me.

The year I turned twenty, I heard about NeuroRestorative, a brain and spinal cord injury recovery center opening in Orlando, about three hours away. The center intrigued me because the founder was a quadriplegic. Mom and I were invited to a fundraising dinner to learn more about the facility and to meet Donna, the woman whose dream was to build this place.

When we told my aunt and uncle in Colorado about this opportunity, they were so excited that my uncle decided he wanted to go with us. We had the date marked, and I couldn't wait to hear Donna's story and learn about the facility. For the first time since my accident, I had a glimmer of hope that this could be the right next step for me.

I was anxious as we made the three-hour drive to Orlando. As we pulled up to the meeting place, a restaurant near the rehab center construction site, the antsy feeling stirring in my stomach intensified.

When my mom, uncle, and I entered the restaurant, a beautiful woman with long blonde hair rolled up to us and introduced herself as Donna. She then presented the man beside her as her husband, Mike. I was a little shocked; I had never entertained the thought of marriage after my injury. Who would want me, a broken girl?

But here I was, meeting a woman with the same brokenness who was married. That night, we were shown the layout for the facility and listened to Donna share her vision for the center. She invited us to have dinner the next evening so we could talk one-on-one.

When we joined Donna and Mike at their favorite restaurant the following night, my mom pulled out my ugly adaptive fork from my backpack and fitted it onto my hand.

“I used to hate having to use those things,” Donna declared.

I looked at her, confused; she had quadriplegia, just like I did. Her fingers didn’t work, just like mine. So why didn’t she have to use these ugly utensils too?

She smiled at me and said, "Here, let me show you a trick."

She picked up a fork and wove its handle between her middle finger and thumb, so her pointer finger rested on top of the handle. She stabbed a piece of chicken on her plate and brought it up to her mouth.

"See? Now you try."

I picked up the fork in front of me and threaded it between my fingers as she had done. When I stabbed one of the raviolis on my plate with more control than I anticipated, then brought it to my mouth, I was elated! It was that simple. I'm sure I wore a goofy smile as I realized, *No more ugly silverware for me!*

The five of us talked for hours, and I was stunned as Donna shared about her life and how she overcame people's preconceived notions about her capabilities following her injury. She had gone to a rehab facility that taught her the necessary skills to live on her own. I had been told people with my injury would *never* be able to live independently. But here was a unicorn—Donna was proof that the "experts" were wrong.

"The rehab facility I went to is no longer in business," she told us, "so I felt called to start a similar one. I want it to be a place where people with spinal cord injuries can experience freedom from the barriers usually associated with that kind of disability.

An added bonus is the man who trained me to live on my own will be the head trainer at this new center."

All this new information was a game changer for me. Ever since I was injured, my family and I were told countless times I would need around-the-clock care. But in one evening, my future drastically expanded, and I could see light instead of darkness when I looked at the road ahead.

On the drive home, my mom and I talked almost nonstop. One thing she said in particular stuck with me.

"I know you always saw yourself going to college, but let's look at this as *your* college." She was right. My friends who had left for college were preparing for their futures. However, this rehabilitation center was my college, and it would prepare me for my own journey.

It was a few months before the facility was completed. Going through the same routine at home every day made me even more eager to get started. I was actually excited about my future!

Unbeknownst to me, those months before I left for Orlando were taxing on my mom. She was nervous about me moving three hours away. One day at work, she was telling a colleague about the facility and how it could equip me with the required skills to live on my own.

"Do you think Katie can put in the work to do it?" he asked. The abruptness of his question startled my mom.

"Of course she can!" she finally responded.

"I only ask because I sensed some hesitation in your voice. And if I can feel it, your daughter will feel it too."

In that moment, my mom realized she needed to let go of her insecurities so they would not become my insecurities.

God not only answered my mom's prayer about my future, but He also sent invaluable nuggets of encouragement—including Donna! Hearing her talk about living independently inspired me to hope again; and my mom's coworker helped her see a potential stumbling block. Both instances made us stronger moving forward.

Now all I needed to do was ask for God's guidance and be open to opportunities as they presented themselves.

To dig deeper into this chapter, turn to page 174 for Discussion Questions.

"All hard work brings a profit, but mere talk leads only to poverty."
~ Proverbs 14:23 (NIV)

"Do not conform to the pattern of this world, but be transformed by the renewing of your mind. Then you will be able to test and approve what God's will is — His good, pleasing, and perfect will."
~ Romans 12:2 (NIV)

CHAPTER SEVEN

BUDDING INDEPENDENCE

The day finally arrived to head off to "college." My family and I drove to a small town called Avalon Park on the outskirts of Orlando. I was delighted to see shops, restaurants, and a grocery store as we pulled into this new community. But I was especially excited when I spotted a coffee shop within rolling distance of the facility. Because of my chronic fatigue, I relied on coffee to prevent me from being a zombie.

Though I was nervous and a little anxious about this new venture, I was most of all grateful for a scholarship Donna and her foundation had gifted me. I would be the first spinal cord injury patient to have therapy at NeuroRestorative. Not only did I want to represent myself and this facility well, but also Donna, who had faith in me.

From the time my family and I walked in the front door of the rehab center, I knew this place was special. Soft hues of yellow, blue, and green colored the walls, which were adorned with modern artwork. It was nothing like the cold, gray hospital setting I had envisioned. The staff greeted us with welcoming smiles and gave us a tour of the kitchen, laundry room, pool, and workout room, which was filled with equipment I barely recognized.

A surge of excitement rippled through me when I noticed silver square buttons embedded with wheelchair symbols next to each door along the hallways. *I will be able to open doors for myself with these buttons!* It may sound silly to be thrilled over a silver button, but I couldn't deny the sense of independence that was beginning to blossom.

As I entered my room, I discovered the walls were painted a soft, happy yellow, and I grinned when I spotted a microwave, a small refrigerator, and sinks that were my level. *I'll be able to use these appliances without assistance!*

I glanced over at my mom, who wore a gentle smile as she watched me take everything in. After she helped me unpack my belongings, we began to hang pictures of my family and friends. Suddenly, a knot in my stomach reminded me how much I was going to miss her.

She had been with me nearly every day since my accident. And she was so much more to me than just my mom—she was my part-time caregiver, my confidante, my compass when I floundered, my biggest cheerleader . . . and my best friend.

Tears rolled down our faces as we hugged each other. But these tears were different from the last time we cried together. These were mingled with a sense of hope.

The following day, I met my new therapists: Terrie, my occupational therapist, had shoulder-length brunette hair and always seemed to be smiling; Lilly was my speech therapist, even though I thought I spoke just fine. My confusion must have been written across my face because she smiled and explained that speech therapy helps with more than just pronouncing words. I was still struggling with my short-term memory, so she and I would be doing exercises to help strengthen my brain.

Next, I was introduced to Jim, the same Rehab Specialist who had trained Donna. He was a rugged but good-looking man, probably in his mid-forties. He had short, white hair with a trimmed beard to match, and his piercing blue eyes seemed genuine and kind. I would be spending most of my time with Jim, and I couldn't wait to start working with him.

Jim and I began our first session later that day in my room.

"Okay, Katie, how about we start with you sharing about your past?" he suggested as he pulled up a stool next to me. "Tell me how you were injured."

Before long, we had covered a wide range of topics. We had a lot of interests in common, and I soon felt like I'd known Jim for years.

His next question was more difficult to answer. "What can you do for yourself?"

I honestly didn't feel as if I could do anything on my own. So I began listing all the things I needed help with: bathing, getting dressed, brushing my hair, and my list went on. He stopped me before I got too far down that rabbit hole.

"I didn't ask about all the things you needed help with; I asked what you feel comfortable doing on your own right now—no matter how small it may seem to you."

I paused as I pushed through all the "I cannot's" in my brain to pick out anything I felt comfortable doing on my own.

"I'm pretty good at using my computer," I said hesitantly.

Although I didn't think that would impress him in the least, I was pleasantly surprised when he exclaimed, "Well, that's a start!"

Just that one question helped reset my mind from focusing on what I could not do to what *I could.*

"Now tell me what you want to accomplish while you're here," he continued, "and what kinds of things you want to learn to do unassisted."

I was suddenly at a loss for words, which truly surprised me. During the months before my arrival, I had created a long list of goals in my head, but now, my mind drew a blank.

I was silent as I considered how to answer him; I didn't know what expectations were realistic for me. So I said the one thing I did know.

"I don't want to rely on another person to do everything for me. I want to be able to live as independently as possible—like Donna."

He grinned. "I like that answer."

We jotted down a list of things I wanted to learn to do without help. First were the less intense tasks like brushing my hair and putting on makeup. We then worked up to bigger things, such as transferring into and out of my wheelchair, doing my own bedtime routine, and even putting on my jeans.

Jim then looked at me solemnly.

"If you are serious about wanting to learn how to do all these things successfully for yourself, it's not going to be easy. We'll work together on finding different ways to accomplish what you want to do, but you will need to put in the time and effort," he advised. "There will be times when you'll want to give up, times when you'll think, "This is impossible," but that's when you'll need to push yourself to keep going. If you're willing to put in the work, you can consider this your boot camp to independence."

I instantly felt as if I were back on the basketball court with my coach. Only now it was Jim giving me the tough love I didn't know I had missed. I finally had a mission, a purpose to get me excited about waking up each morning. My competitive nature kicked in.

"I'll do whatever it takes to accomplish my independence," I assured him.

With a twinkle in his eye, Jim said, "Get some rest then; boot camp starts in the morning."

We began with the first tasks on my list: finding ways to brush my hair and do my makeup.

Just like using a fork the way Donna showed me, I mixed a little creativity and imagination into how to hold things and/or use adaptations. If one way didn't work, Jim and I put our heads together to figure out a way that did.

"There are so many different ways to do the same thing, you just have to figure out the best way for you," Jim often reminded me. "It doesn't matter how awkward or silly you look doing it. As long as you can get it done, that's your way."

That's what I liked most about Jim. He didn't classify what I could do based on my injury; rather, he helped me think outside the box to figure out ways that worked for me.

As we began tackling transfers and learning how to put on my jeans, things got more challenging. It took me two hours the first time I put on my jeans! I was utterly exhausted when they were finally over my hips, but I was ecstatic to conquer something I had once deemed impossible. Jim was right—learning to do things that would change how I lived would not be easy.

Building up the muscles in my shoulders and arms was vital so I could lift myself, pull myself up in bed, and so on. Those foreign-looking machines in the weight room became oh-so familiar. Interestingly enough, my legs were the heaviest weights for me to lift because of their spasticity. When I used my arms to lift a leg, more times than not, it would pull back down in protest.

That made me even more determined to work harder in the gym, because I knew what I was up against outside the weight room. This rigorous training made me hurt in places I didn't even know had feeling!

But there were also times I just wanted to quit. The instant this familiar feeling surfaced, I would be taken back to my days on the basketball court. I remember numerous practices where I wanted to give up because I didn't think my body could endure any more strenuous (and what felt like cruel) training.

I hated one drill in particular—suicides—and they were called that for good reason! My team would line up on the baseline under the hoop, and when the coach blew his whistle, we would sprint to the first foul line, touch it, and then sprint back to the start. Next, sprint to the half-court line, touch it, then sprint back to the start. We would continue this exercise with sprints to the opposite foul line and then the opposite baseline, running back to the start after each one.

Every time I reached down to touch the lines, my body wanted to fall to the floor and stay there. However, I willed myself to keep going, even when my brain told me it wasn't possible. We would do several of these drills after intense practices. By the time we finished, the team wanted to collapse.

But here's the thing. Those drills made me stronger during games. And I knew my training with Jim was leading me to a future of self-reliance. So, I kept going, even when my body and brain fought back.

After several weeks of intense conditioning, I was both mentally and physically tired, just as Jim had warned. I was especially discouraged because I couldn't recall the steps correctly to transfer myself into bed. My occupational therapist and I had hung signs around my room to help me remember how to complete different tasks, so we did this for my transfer to bed as well.

I would parallel park my wheelchair on the right side of the bed, then look at the list of steps on the wall beside me. After I ensured everything was in the right position, I put on my chest strap, which securely held the top half of my body to the chair. Next, I swung my left armrest out of the way. Referencing the list again, I'd lift my left leg onto the bed, then cross my right leg over the top of it. I then released the chest strap so I could swing my arms and use that momentum to twist my top half with enough force to roll onto the bed.

With this spurt of energy, I was supposed to do a complete roll onto the bed, ending up on my back. Instead, I would find myself stuck, lying on my stomach halfway through the roll. This transfer sounded simple enough to do, which is why it frustrated me so much when I couldn't complete it.

Jim saw my discouragement, so one evening he asked me to follow him into another room.

"If you aren't able to transfer yourself, we'll need to think of a different solution—and this is it."

Set up in the room was a Hoyer lift above a bed. Tears started streaming down my face as I stared at the apparatus. *If I need to rely on a Hoyer lift to get me into bed, I'll be limited in my independence.*

Jim placed me in the sling for the Hoyer and operated the controls as it lifted me out of my wheelchair and set me on the bed. I cried throughout the entire process, and I quickly decided that depending on another person, yet again, to get me in and out of bed was not an option.

I didn't say much to Jim after we finished, but I was more motivated than ever. I was at this facility to learn how to do things on my own, and I was determined to transfer into bed without relying on anything or anyone! Most of that night, I practiced the steps to roll myself into bed. I got stuck more often than not and was grateful a caretaker was standing by to help me.

After numerous attempts, I finally got it! I continued practicing, and the more I repeated the steps, the easier they became. I realized then that my mindset was instrumental in determining whether I succeeded or failed. I not only had to *want* to prevail, but I also had to believe that I *could* prevail if I made the effort.

One of the things I enjoyed most at NeuroRestorative were my fellow patients. It wasn't hard to create friendships since most of us had the same goal: to better equip ourselves for the future. At the end of each day, we would gather in the common area to eat dinner and share events from our day.

One evening, I quietly looked around at the people in that room. While they all were classified with the same ailment, each individual had a hardship he or she was battling to create a new normal. I observed firsthand how the term "brain injury" can be so broad—from completely transforming a person's livelihood to struggling with memory issues. I took myself out of my shoes for a while and considered how each person's brain injury was affecting his or her life.

A man in his late thirties was working hard to take steps with a walker and to form words that were intelligible; he usually ended up discouraged. He could no longer take care of himself, let alone his wife and young child, who visited him often. I tried to imagine how I would feel if I were once the head of the household and, in an instant, could no longer provide for my family. I also am quite the talker, so I couldn't imagine the frustration of being unable to communicate.

I loved having conversations with a vibrant, charismatic woman who was excited for everything in life. Our chats sometimes came to an abrupt halt because of her confusion, but that didn't stop me from wanting to experience her zesty way of explaining things.

It was particularly heart-wrenching to watch people go through this challenging time without family, friends, or visitors to support them. I encountered so many versions of the same story of brokenness—where a person's life was shattered in the blink of an eye—living under one roof.

I began viewing my own situation through a different lens; in the grand scheme of things, it wasn't that bad. I was blessed to have family and friends who loved and supported me. And though my body was broken, my brain injury wasn't nearly as bad as the trauma surgeon had predicted when he suggested taking me off life support.

But that was just it! Given everything my brain had endured—lack of oxygen, blunt force trauma, thrashing about inside my skull—the effects should've been much more significant. As I watched other patients battle to form words or even make eye contact, I realized God had spared me, for whatever reason, from a more severe brain injury. I was only struggling with short-term memory issues and chronic fatigue. Even though I still had my "Why me?" breakdowns, I began to see glimmers of God's grace.

After seven months at NeuroRestorative, I left feeling physically and mentally stronger. Any physical obstacles I confronted were seen as opportunities rather than barriers. Most of all, my heart was overflowing with hope for the future.

And I began to see my life truly was a gift.

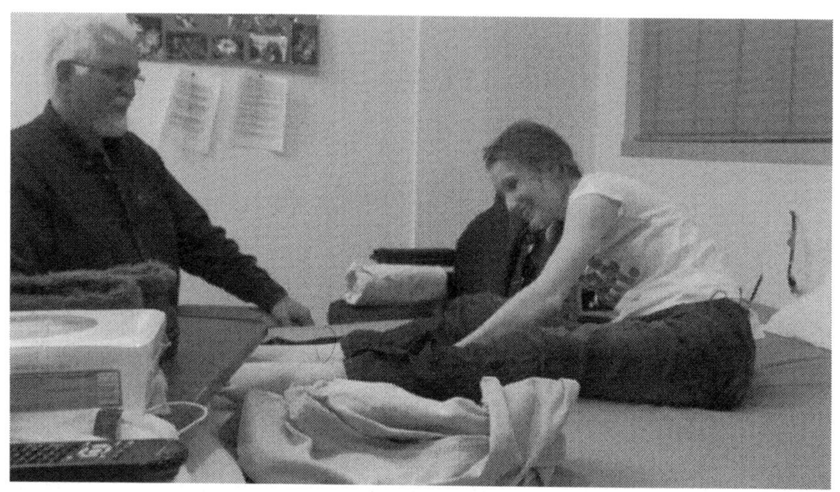

To dig deeper into this chapter, turn to page 175 for Discussion Questions.

"Do not be overcome by evil, but overcome evil with good."
~ Romans 12:21 (NKJV)

"And we know that in all things God works for the good of those who love Him, who have been called according to His purpose."
~ Romans 8:28 (NIV)

CHAPTER EIGHT

HEALING THROUGH THE PAIN

I must admit that sometimes when God opens a door, He catches me completely off guard!

That was the case when my occupational and speech therapists at NeuroRestorative came bubbling into my room one day with so much enthusiasm, I was overwhelmed before they said a word. Terrie and Lilly informed me of an upcoming Miss Wheelchair Florida pageant in Tampa (about ninety minutes away).

"I really don't feel like wheeling around in my swimsuit in front of judges," I shrugged sarcastically.

Terrie gave me a sly smirk as Lilly proceeded to explain this pageant wasn't like that.

"Miss Wheelchair Florida is more of an advocacy role for people with different abilities," she told me.

Now that was something I could get behind! After all, wasn't I already advocating for a better future for myself? And I really wanted to find a way to pay it forward for others, just as Donna had done for me.

I called my mom to tell her about this opportunity; I was a little shocked when she was all for it. I had almost forgotten she competed nationally in the Junior Miss Pageant when she was eighteen, representing her home state of Wyoming. My mom has always been outgoing and sporty, nothing like the stereotypical, uptight pageant queens the movies portray. Her spunky personality and strong will landed her among the top five finalists in that competition.

She began reminiscing about her fond memories from her pageant days, and I started warming up to the idea of entering one myself. My competitive nature surfaced once again. I guess this pageant business was more in my blood than I thought!

To compete for Miss Wheelchair Florida, I needed a platform—something I was passionate about bringing to light. Mom and I discussed various topics, but none felt right.

Then she said something that struck a chord: "How about focusing on the reason you are in a wheelchair?"

Immediately, my body tensed up. Having to relive that night of bad decisions put a knot in my stomach. I didn't even like to speak about the crash with the people closest to me, let alone broadcast it to an audience I didn't even know. I was embarrassed and ashamed that something I chose to do drastically altered my life and caused the people I loved to change the way they lived too.

But there was also another reason: Chelsea. After I returned home from the hospital, I was told Chelsea had stopped playing basketball—not only because of her leg injury, but also because I wasn't on the court with her anymore. She had waited five months for me to get home so she could ask my permission to play basketball again.

"Of course, I want you to keep playing! We can't both be paralyzed," I told her as we embraced, tears trickling down our cheeks. She was already living with so much guilt, I worried how she would feel if I used the accident as a platform. Neither of us set out that night to jeopardize our lives. Yet, here I was, considering whether to purposely recount the night we both wished had never happened.

As I debated the pros and cons of the wreck as a platform, I began to realize many factors played a role in our crash. We were driving late at night, we had the music turned up, we were being given directions off my speakerphone, and our minds were on the party instead of on the road. I then thought about how many times similar scenarios had played out in my past.

More often than not, my friends and I were preoccupied with teenage matters, and driving was just another thing amidst all the other things. Rarely was driving our sole focus. And it dawned on me that this crash could have happened multiple times before it actually occurred.

I now felt an urgency to share about the dangers of distracted driving. If our story could prevent just one person from suffering a similar fate, it didn't matter how uncomfortable it made me. For the first time in four years, I figured out how to recycle that night of pain and bad decisions into a cautionary tale for good.

I had found my platform.

I started doing lots of research for my presentation on the dangers of distracted driving. The more I learned, the more I realized how blessed I was to still be alive. According to the National Highway Traffic Safety Administration, 32,092 people were killed, and 2.3 million victims were injured the same year my life hung in the balance.[2]

2 US Department of Transportation 2006. "Traffic Safety Facts 2006: A Compilation of Motor Vehicle Crash Data From The Fatality Analysis Reporting System and The General Estimates System.

As I thought about all those people who were hurt, I couldn't help but wonder how their injuries affected their lives. The more I studied that number, the more real this subject became. Each of those numbers was a living, breathing human being. *I was one of those numbers.*

My passion for this topic grew. I was going to share my story for those 32,092 lives who were lost that year and for the 2.3 million who were injured. I sincerely hoped those who heard what happened to me would consider their actions while in a vehicle. I was determined to do everything I could to help prevent other lives from becoming a future statistic.

It was almost time for my mom and me to make our way to Tampa when someone from the pageant called. Since I was only twenty years old, I was a year too young to participate. My heart sank, but then she presented another idea.

"Katie, you can still compete, and if you match or better the winner's score, you will become Florida's first Junior Miss Wheelchair. You just won't be able to compete nationally."

Not participating nationally didn't bother me. I just wanted a chance to share what I had learned about the dangers of distracted driving.

In high school, when guest speakers told us how distracted driving could permanently alter or end a person's life, I was the girl sitting in the back thinking, *Yeah, but what are the chances of something like that actually happening to me?* I had to learn the hard way that those chances were far greater than I anticipated. I aimed to use my story of brokenness to shed light on the importance of focusing on the road while behind the wheel, as well as the importance of being a respectful passenger.

I was excited the day my mom, my four-year-old brother, and I headed to Tampa. I felt elegant in a beaded purple gown with my long brown hair styled in a simple yet classy updo. I wasn't used to feeling this glamorous, but it was a nice change from the workout queen I'd become at the rehab facility.

We arrived early so I could talk with a few of the contestants about their lives and what motivated them to do this pageant. They all looked stunning in their gowns while sitting in their wheelchairs. Each woman I spoke with was inspiring in her own way. It made me more eager to share my passion, as well as hear these strong individuals advocate for issues near and dear to their hearts.

After we all presented our platforms, the judges asked each of us a series of questions. These were based on our character and why we had chosen our particular platform. Toward the end of the pageant, I noticed my cheeks were starting to hurt from the genuine smile I had worn all evening. Miss Wheelchair Florida was nothing like the stereotypical pageant I had first imagined, and I was thankful for that.

I cheered loudly as the winner was being crowned. I had talked with this particular woman before the pageant began. Her topic of domestic abuse was personal, painful, yet inspiring. She was strong in her conviction and endearing about her desire to help other women in similar circumstances become advocates for themselves.

Something unique also took place during that pageant. The first Junior Miss Wheelchair Florida was announced . . . me! As one of the judges placed a crown on my head and handed me a bouquet of roses, my little brother, Carson, ran out of the crowd to give me a huge hug. I honestly hadn't expected to enjoy the pageant experience as much as I did. I not only got to share all I had learned about distracted driving, but I also grew in my understanding of the issues these powerful women championed.

Soon after the pageant, I was invited to share my presentation at an Abilities Expo; I eagerly accepted. When my former high school heard I was speaking on the dangers of distracted driving, they asked if I would come share my message with the student body during their annual safe driving program.

Although I was nervous, I was also grateful for this opportunity and even more thankful that I had several months to prepare. None of us could have predicted the timeliness of my presentation. Two weeks before I was scheduled to speak, five teenagers were killed in two car crashes in the county where I had spent a large part of my childhood.

As my mom and I pulled into my alma mater's parking lot, we were greeted by a heap of contorted metal that once was a car. It further emphasized the importance of convincing these teenagers that being behind the wheel of a two-ton vehicle was more than just a privilege; it was one of the most significant responsibilities they could have.

I passionately shared my story of how distracted driving drastically changed my life . . . forever. I showed photos from my days on the basketball team, being at the beach with friends, and moments from my life as a typical teen—much like those listening to me. But the pictures and my story changed in a split second.

My once animated face now appeared lifeless as I lay in a hospital bed, on oxygen, with a metal halo fastened to my skull and shoulders to keep my neck securely in place. This photo was taken five weeks after my crash as I was being medically airlifted to the rehab hospital in Colorado.

It was the first picture my mom had the courage to take after my near-death experience. Hope had begun to flicker as the aircraft soared away from the ICU. Still, the once fun-loving, chatty, social butterfly was no longer recognizable.

I described my challenges and frustrations with moving home and being totally dependent on another person for *everything*. Graphics illustrated my research on how frequently crashes occur due to distractions in the car. I prayed these sobering statistics would have an impact on these students; I didn't want them to have the same invincible mindset I once had.

A few local news stations interviewed me following my presentation. It was emotionally draining to relive those horrific moments of my life, but the positive responses I received motivated me to keep sharing my story. If I could get one young person to stop and think before getting behind the wheel, it was worth it.

A short time later, I received a call from a woman named Charlene at the National Safety Council's headquarters in Illinois.

"Hi, Katie! I've been trying to get hold of you ever since I saw a news broadcast about your speech to high school students. A team here at the Safety Council is raising awareness regarding the dangers of distracted driving. Would you be interested in volunteering to speak on the subject as part of our initiative?" she asked.

Wow! I couldn't believe I was receiving an opportunity to share about my passion on a national level! As Charlene and I continued our conversation, she began telling me her reason for becoming the administrator of this team. I hung on every word as she shared about her father and how he was killed by a distracted driver.

I couldn't fathom how devastating it must have been to suddenly lose her beloved father. But I admired her for searching for the good that could come out of tragedy. In fact, instead of sorrow crippling her, it was the very thing that fueled her. Charlene disclosed that each team member had his or her own experience of loss or brokenness because of distracted driving. She assured me they were just as passionate as she was about sharing their story to raise awareness.

After Charlene and I ended our call, I started thinking about my renewed life and my changed attitude. I once was ashamed of why I was living as a quadriplegic. I would never have considered sitting on a stage and voluntarily reliving that night of lies and poor choices in front of hundreds of people.

But that was the beauty of God's plan. My way would have been to keep the reasons for that car crash hidden in my heart—but that wouldn't have benefited anyone. Here God was, opening door after door for me to use my story as a cautionary tale. And now I was being given a national platform to shine a light on my bad decisions in hopes of keeping someone else from the same fate.

Every time I shared my story, something happened that's hard to put into words. I expected to be uncomfortable reliving that pain, but what I didn't anticipate was my own healing. It was as if I were being stitched back together emotionally with every word, knowing I had the potential to affect another person's outcome.

God really does work in mysterious ways. The very part of my life I once wished I could delete had now become my purpose. It allowed me to speak to hundreds of young people about the dangers of distracted driving. I am so grateful for that night my mom and I prayed, committing my future to God's hands. He had been leading me each step of the way—even if I couldn't see it then.

God can and does recycle, even the parts of our lives we are ashamed of and try to keep private. He turns it all into good, not only for us but also for others . . . we just have to allow Him access.

To dig deeper into this chapter, turn to page 177 for Discussion Questions.

"But those who wait on the Lord shall renew their strength; they shall mount up with wings like eagles, they shall run and not be weary, they shall walk and not faint." ~ Isaiah 40:31 (NKJV)

"Our help is in the name of the Lord, the Maker of heaven and earth." ~ Psalm 124:8 (NIV)

CHAPTER NINE

SPREADING MY WINGS

The time had come for me to take the knowledge I gained at NeuroRestorative and begin the next chapter in my journey to independence—venturing out on my own.

Apartment searching was a little different for me because I had to consider how I could do things for myself from a seated position. My new home would require a roll-in shower, a pantry for food storage since I couldn't reach the cabinets, and a front-loading washer and dryer.

Jim helped my mom and me find an apartment with the right specifications and aided us in modifying a few things, such as handle extenders for my sinks so I could reach them. My apartment was in a great location: near the rehab facility and close to where Jim lived. I still attended therapy a few times a week, so I was able to take a wheelchair-accessible bus to and from my NeuroRestorative appointments.

I was twenty-one now and enjoying my newfound freedom, but the biggest challenge was living three hours away from my family. My mom and Carson came to visit every chance they got, but the time we spent together never seemed to be enough. Jim knew I missed my family, so he and his family became a great source of comfort to me as well as my mom, who was grateful I had someone looking out for me while I created a new normal for myself in Orlando.

I was much more self-sufficient after my intense training, but I still needed a caregiver for a few hours in the mornings to help me get up and get ready. Once again, I was blessed to find reliable and friendly women to help me. While I was grateful for their assistance, I also welcomed time by myself when I was free to figure things out independently.

Not long after I moved in, I faced my first obstacle. I was reading an excellent book; of course, I dropped it on the floor amid a pivotal plot twist. I was totally absorbed in this story and got frustrated that the answers to what happened next were just beyond my grasp. I sat and thought about what Jim might tell me.

"There are so many different ways to do the same thing; you just have to figure out your way." As soon as those familiar words echoed in my mind, I began to smile. *Of course! Just because I can't reach down with my hand and get the book doesn't mean I can't get it up off the floor some other way.*

It hadn't taken Jim long to discover I have the special gift of klutziness. Unfortunately, I can't blame it on my injury—I've always had a knack for fumbling objects! He had shown me how to stretch out a wire clothes hanger to retrieve items I dropped or that were out of my reach.

The trick was to put my wrist through the oval shape of the stretched-out hanger and use the hook part to snare loops I had attached to remote controls or anything else I frequently dropped. The problem was I didn't have a loop attached to the back of the book! I glanced around my apartment for something I could sweep the book into and pick up.

I first tried a baseball cap, but after several failed attempts, I looked around for something sturdier. I spotted a basket on a nearby table, so I dropped it on the floor and swept the book into it. I then hooked the handle with the clothes hanger and hoisted them both up into my lap. This whole process took over an hour, but I didn't care. I had successfully rescued my book . . . all by myself!

I was so excited, I forgot all about the plot twist and immediately called Jim to share my moment of triumph. I was beaming with pride, and I could hear the smile in Jim's voice as he asked questions about my thought process in figuring out what to do next. This was the first time I had accomplished a seemingly impossible feat without needing help or advice from another person. In my elation, I eagerly called most of my family to declare my story of victory.

The rehab center in Orlando truly was my "college" during that point in my life. It was my necessary step forward in discovering who I was and having confidence in whom I ultimately could become.

One thing I quickly realized about living alone—no matter how self-sufficient I wanted to be, I still needed help. On more than one occasion, I got stuck while rolling into bed. With no one there to assist me, I'd cry out, "God, help!" More often than not, I'd feel a gentle nudge helping me to roll all the way into bed.

Other times, I'd have an unexplainable surge of energy that gave me the strength to push myself over. And sometimes, I was overwhelmed with a sense of peace, which allowed me to rest before figuring out how to complete the transfer. I began to get a little more comfortable with God, knowing He was always with me, even if I hadn't completely forgiven Him.

I'd been living in my apartment for almost a year when my mom called to say Brian had received a job offer in Texas. They decided it would be a good opportunity, so the family was moving in a few months. She took a deep breath before she spoke again.

"Katie, I know you're creating a life for yourself in Orlando, so you don't have to move with us if you don't want to."

That whole time I was thinking about how much I already missed her, living three hours away and only seeing her occasionally. As soon as she stopped talking, I was ready with my response:

"I think I'll fit in quite nicely in the Lone Star State."

I heard her sigh of relief as she started laughing. "I know you will!"

Brian and Carson drove ahead of us with a U-Haul containing the contents of our lives. We made a pit stop in Louisiana for a real Cajun experience. We chowed down on authentic jambalaya and laughed as we watched Carson pull the heads off crawfish before slurping them down. As we crossed the border into Texas, my mom and I started jamming out to good old country music. We passed the time by making a game of how many trucks we could count around us.

I'm going to like it here! I decided.

To dig deeper into this chapter, turn to page 179 for Discussion Questions.

"O God, we meditate on your unfailing love." ~ Psalm 48:9a (NLT)

CHAPTER TEN

THIS AIN'T MY FIRST RODEO

Mom and Brian knew I wanted to maintain the independence I had worked so hard to gain. They wanted that for me, too, so we began to search for a community where I could thrive. Staying active is important to me, so finding an apartment with places within wheeling distance was a must. In the meantime, I enjoyed living with my family once again.

Carson Jett was now a young boy who absolutely loved being outside. Swimming in the pool was where you could find him most days. I delighted in viewing the world through the eyes of an adolescent boy and all the things he found awesome.

One day, he and Brian brought home a turtle they found on their way home. We had a fountain outside our house that contained tadpoles, and Carson thought they and the turtle would make great friends. To our surprise, that turtle was a fast one! Carson did his best to keep bringing him home, but the shelled speedster didn't end up staying with us for long.

I swiftly discovered country music wasn't the only thing popular in our part of Texas. Warmhearted people extended Southern hospitality to everyone, including strangers. Opening a door for someone or saying, "God bless you" and "Bless your heart!" were everyday occurrences.

My family and I were invited to church a few times during our four years in Texas. The charismatic worship and outpouring of faith weren't things I was used to at all! It was quite different from the Catholic services I attended in my younger years. Even though we only attended a few times, the people were so friendly and kind, it felt like being in church even outside the walls.

My family and I eventually found a little community that fit my criteria about fifteen minutes away from Mom and Brian's home. It featured restaurants, a movie theater, and a trail along the waterway. It even had a wheelchair-accessible trolley that stopped at the grocery store. It was perfect! Now we just needed to find the right apartment.

The first apartment building we visited was close to everything; unfortunately, the doors were so heavy, I could not open them on my own. We continued looking and located a wonderful apartment complex just a little further away. This was where I made my new home.

Shortly before I moved, my mom and I began searching for a caregiver to help me a couple of hours each morning. It took some trial and error before we finally found the right person. I was nervous as I lay in bed the morning I was to meet her. I wondered what she would be like, if she'd be around my age, and more than anything, if we'd get along. When she opened the door to my bedroom, I immediately noticed her contagious smile, and my anxiety melted away.

Asha had noticed on my paperwork we were the same age. We spent some time getting to know each other, then I outlined what needed to be done for my care routine. While I'm aware everyone has his or her own way of doing things, I'm always grateful my caregivers are willing to learn the system I've found works for me.

I learned how to instruct others on doing things my way while at NeuroRestorative. Honestly, I may have gotten a little *too* good at it, because periodically I found myself telling my mom or dad just how things should be done. They'd give me *that* look—you know the one I'm talking about—and I'd quickly remember they didn't need my instruction; they were pros by now.

As Asha became more comfortable with me and my morning routine, she confided that she had been nervous the first day. She had never taken care of someone with paralysis before. But we were an awesome team for several years. Once she became pregnant, Asha retired from her role as caregiver and settled for being one of my best friends. She even asked me to be the godmother of her beautiful baby girl. To say I felt blessed is an understatement.

Prior to my accident, I had never imagined needing help to get ready each day. But once again, God showed up in the details and placed amazing caregivers in my life so I could live as normally as possible. These women became some of my greatest friends, and I probably would have never met them if it weren't for this broken body.

Now that I was in Texas, I didn't want to regress after working so hard mentally and physically at the facility in Orlando. I looked online for a place where I could continue my physical therapy. I found one nearby, and my brother Jeff, who was visiting, drove me over to check it out.

We met with an occupational therapist to develop a game plan. After reviewing my information, she wanted to know more about me and what I wanted to accomplish. I chronicled my injury and the transitional living facility I had gone to in Florida. I explained that I had recently moved here and wanted to maintain my strength.

She nodded and then asked a familiar question. "What kinds of things can you do for yourself?"

I didn't waste time telling her everything I had learned with Jim. But when I mentioned I was able to get my pants on by myself, she stopped me and gave me a pitiful smile.

"Katie, you don't have to try to impress me. I can see your level of injury right here," she said, pointing to my paperwork.

Jeff's eyes widened at this, but I smiled and asked if she wanted me to show her. My response must have shocked her because it took her a while to consent.

I rolled over to a mat that was the right height for my wheelchair. Jeff took my bed ladder, which is basically a long rope with many loops I can hook my arms in, and tied it to the middle leg of the table underneath the mat. The bed ladder allows me to pull myself up and stabilize as I move myself around, plus it grants me complete mobility in bed. I also happened to bring along pants with the pull-up straps Jim made for me.

Once we were all set up, I lifted my legs onto the mat and did my roll-in transfer. I used the bed ladder to maneuver myself around enough to take my pants off—in front of everyone in the room. Lying on the mat in my underwear, I proceeded to put on the pants with the pull-up straps. After I returned to my chair, I accepted the occupational therapist's apology. I realized I had all the therapy I needed just doing my everyday routine.

But that didn't mean my family and I stopped trying to invent ways to do things a little easier. For example, when I traveled, I used my manual wheelchair with power-assisted wheels. Taking my 400-pound electric wheelchair on an airplane wasn't really feasible. Still, my manual wheelchair and I didn't get along too well. My dad came up with an idea to help with my proficiency.

We practiced in the parking lot of a nearby school, where he lined up cones several feet apart. Then, he'd time me as I wove in and out of the cones, making my way toward him. Dad always has a way of igniting my competitive streak! Again and again, I went as fast as I could, always trying to beat my previous time. Disclaimer: the times weren't very impressive, but I was determined to keep getting better!

A couple of the residual effects of my brain injury continued to plague me: chronic fatigue and short-term memory loss. Even with medication and coffee, at times I still felt as if I were a zombie just rolling through my days. My doctor and I tried to find the proper drugs, but either the side effects were worse than the ailment, or the medication only worked intermittently.

I finally decided to try meditation. My mom had recommended it in the past, and I even tried it a few times, but I now needed to be serious about it. I didn't want to keep piling up medications on an already extensive list.

Every day around 3:00 p.m., I was so exhausted, I wanted to get in bed and not get up until the following day. So, I decided this was the best time to meditate. I had no idea how to start, but I went into my bedroom, turned the lights off, and began taking deep breaths in through my nose and out through my mouth. It was such a nice release to just be still and relax.

I had never realized the sound of silence could be so soothing. I was accustomed to having background noise during my day—whether it was music playing or a TV show. But the deeper I breathed and focused on my breath, the more oblivious I became to noises. Even if I wasn't meditating the "right" way, it worked for me. Whether I sat in silence for ten minutes or an hour, I could recharge for the rest of the day.

A surprising aftereffect of my meditation was the healing that came with the silence I sought. After practicing meditation for many years, I was able to come off medications that used to keep me awake; my short-term memory seemed to substantially improve as well. I even started helping other people remember things instead of vice versa!

Opportunities for sharing my story continued to present themselves. An organization called FCCLA (Family, Career, and Community Leaders of America) contacted me about possibly traveling around the state to speak with their teenage members. The nonprofit promotes personal growth and leadership development for young men and women.

After I spoke with one of the directors, she invited me to their state leadership meeting in Dallas. She explained the speech I presented there would determine whether they wanted me to share my story the following year.

My mom and I made the five-hour drive to Dallas so I could address 1,000 teenage FCCLA members. During my presentation, my mom used the screen behind me to show slides including the mangled car, me in a coma, and sobering statistics. I spoke passionately as I looked out and saw myself in their young, unassuming eyes.

After I poured out my heart, numerous teens came up to me with promises of becoming better drivers and passengers alike. The FCCLA asked me to speak at eight of their meetings with locations scattered across Texas.

I was so excited to begin this journey, but after the first few cities, I realized it wasn't what I imagined. Instead of a room full of students like I'd experienced in Dallas, I discovered my presentation was just an option for students amid all the other events. Only a handful of students attended in each city, and I began to wonder if it was worth the effort my mom and I put into it. Traveling and overnight stays for me are not easy.

When I am away from the comfort of my home, I fully rely on another person to take care of me.

My mom had graciously agreed to take time off work to be with me. She was my chauffeur, caregiver, secretary, makeup and hair stylist, and, most importantly, my confidante during these times of travel. I felt guilty taking her away from her job when just a few students would show up, but she always assured me she would do it a hundred times over. Regardless, I felt like I wasn't reaching anyone, and my mom missing work gnawed at me.

At my second to last FCCLA conference, I spoke to more faculty members than students. As my mom and I were leaving the auditorium, my spirits were low until a cardboard diorama caught my eye. It was in the shape of a car with a license plate that said, "Drive Safe." I smiled as I kept rolling toward the door. A few minutes later, the girls with the diorama approached me.

"Are you Katie Mathews?"

I was caught off guard, so I just nodded.

"A year ago, we attended your speech at the Dallas FCCLA meeting, and it inspired us to do a presentation on the dangers of distracted driving."

The girls escorted me back to their diorama. When they opened the car, there were pictures of many stories, including mine, among the research they had compiled. These teenagers, who had heard my story months ago, piggybacked off of my passion and created their own presentation in hopes of preventing another dreadful crash. God knew I needed a nudge of encouragement, and he used these girls to feed my soul.

My final FCCLA speech was canceled because of unusually bad weather in that location, so they asked me to share my story at a high school instead. It so happened I was scheduled to address the students on the eighth anniversary of my crash. I knew this wasn't a coincidence, so my mom and I headed to the high school with more zeal than ever.

I shared my message with about 300 sophomores that afternoon. On the drive home, I had a revelation. Somewhere along the way, I had forgotten it wasn't about the number of students in the room—it was about the potential my story had to be a beacon, whether for one person or 100. I'll probably never know how hearing about my accident and its consequences affected the lives of others, but God knows . . . and that's all that matters.

To dig deeper into this chapter, turn to page 181 for Discussion Questions.

"But be sure to fear the Lord and faithfully serve Him. Think of all the wonderful things He has done for you." ~ 1 Samuel 12:24 (NLT)

CHAPTER ELEVEN

A COWBOY COMES TO TOWN

Dogs have always been a big part of our family. Abbie ultimately chose my mom as her person, but she was still by my side from kindergarten through my senior year of high school. Abbie lived through a lot with us, and she never strayed far from my mom and me. She was wonderful, loyal, and loving; being around her always comforted my heart.

After Abbie passed away, my mom encouraged me to apply for a service dog. Taking care of my needs was already a lot, and I imagined the added chores of a dog would be more than my caregivers and I could handle. I also got it in my head that having a service dog would bring more attention to the fact that I was in a wheelchair.

So, every time my mom brought up the subject, I would say no. It wasn't until I moved into my own apartment that I realized living independently was, in fact, a bit lonely. I began to entertain the idea of a helpful, four-legged friend.

My mom and I began to research places in Texas that trained service dogs to help people living with mobility impairments. I was completely baffled by the length of the waitlists to be paired with a dog—it was usually at least two years. When I came across a website that guaranteed me a service dog within six months, I immediately called the number.

I spoke to a woman who told me she was the trainer and that she would be doing a presentation with her dogs at an event. She invited my mom and me to come meet her and observe her training techniques. Unfortunately, my mom and I didn't feel comfortable with the harsh way she trained her dogs. We both agreed we should keep looking.

With settling into my new apartment and the general busyness of life, the service dog search was put on the back burner until I gave a speech about distracted driving to a group of teenage girls. My mom's friend had assembled this group of girls, which included her daughter. Following my presentation, I asked if there were any questions.

"Do you want a service dog?" one of the girls inquired.

My mom smiled and said, "Yes! We talked about applying for one when we first moved here, but we need to start looking into places again to get Katie's name on the waitlist."

Nothing further was said, but my mom's friend took it to heart. After doing some research, she found an organization that adopts shelter dogs and trains them to be service dogs. She passed along the information to my mom, who shared it with me.

As soon as I opened up Service Dogs, Inc.'s website, I started to smile. I loved all the happy pictures and gleeful testimonies of people with their pups following graduation. But what really caught my eye was the mention of positive training methods. I am a huge believer in positive reinforcement over negativity. And my heart was full when I saw they rescued shelter dogs and trained them to become service dogs.

I continued exploring the website and breathed a sigh of relief when I read the training of my potential service dog would be at no cost to me. Generous donations covered all the expenses of training. I excitedly filled out an application. Not long afterward, I got a call back from Service Dogs, Inc. and was told there was already a long waitlist. However, they reassured me my name had been added, and I would be notified as soon as it was my turn.

Several months later, Service Dogs, Inc. informed me I was at the top of their list. They wanted to set up an interview so the trainers could get to know me and my expectations for a service dog. My mom and I eagerly made the three-hour drive to their headquarters in Dripping Springs. My stomach was filled with butterflies when we arrived, but I instantly broke into a smile when I saw genuine happiness radiating off the staff. I took that as a good sign.

I'm not sure why, but I felt nervous during my interview with the owner and head trainers. It was obvious this company was serious about matching dogs with people who were willing to put in the time and effort to create a successful partnership. I wanted them to see I was totally committed to nurturing a strong bond with my own service dog. Plus, once I have my heart set on something, I work as hard as possible to make it a reality.

I was ecstatic when the trainers told me I was a good candidate for one of their dogs. Since they were still in the midst of training, they were to notify me when it was time to pair me with a dog. As soon as I got home, I scoured their website and social media pages in hopes of seeing dogs they were training. To my delight, I found photos of the current class. When I saw the handsome face of a chocolate lab named Cowboy, I immediately fell in love. There was just one catch; I didn't get to choose my dog.

When I got the call, my mom and I headed back to Dripping Springs to meet my new partner. The trainers had selected several dogs they thought were good candidates. My interactions with each dog would be videotaped, and the trainers would then determine which dog was best for me.

They reiterated that the dog chooses the human, not the other way around.

At first, I was a bit perplexed as to how the trainers could tell if a dog chose me. But once I started going through the process, it all made sense. It didn't matter what I thought; if the dog wasn't excited to work with me, there was no partnership. Every dog I met was wonderful; but with each new wagging tail, my hope of Cowboy being in this group got smaller and smaller.

I was on cloud nine when Cowboy came in as the last potential candidate. I was so excited at the sight of him, I probably made a fool of myself. I glanced over at my mom, and happy tears were rolling down her cheeks. She was videotaping all the possible service dog matches on her phone so our family could be part of this process.

As soon as I composed myself, I repeated the commands I had given the other potential partners. But this time was different. I already felt a connection with this handsome boy; a few days later, I got the call that Cowboy had chosen me too.

Over the next few months, trainers tailored Cowboy's skillset to my specific needs. He learned how to pull open doors with a rope, tug my clothing off, and retrieve dropped items from the floor and place them in my lap. As we all know, that was a skill I would appreciate daily!

Once the trainers were confident in Cowboy's abilities, I went back to headquarters so we could train together. The head trainer cautioned me that I would be exhausted from everything I was learning, as well as the emotional aspect of nurturing this new bond with Cowboy. And oh boy, was he right! It didn't take long for me to discover I was the one who needed this training so I could be brought up to Cowboy's level.

I'd spent the last seven years learning how to maneuver my wheelchair, and now I needed to be aware of a four-legged being who would share my space. We practiced numerous obstacle courses so Cowboy and I could work on functional exercises together. One of the most interesting was his jumping in front of me so we both could squeeze through narrow doorways or halls.

When I asked why they would teach a dog to walk backward, I was given an obvious answer.

"If you're going through a narrow doorway with a heavy door that shuts behind you, this prevents Cowboy from getting caught in the door when it shuts." His walking backward also helped us get up ramps without my worrying his leash would get caught under my wheels.

Cowboy should be given more kudos because, while doing all these exercises, he had to familiarize himself with how I drive.

This was not an easy task! If I'd had to take a driving test to get my power wheelchair, I'm not sure I would have passed. Granted, over the years, I've gotten better with my driving; but now that I had a helper attached to me, I needed to be mindful of my whereabouts. Believe it or not, that took a lot of extra energy.

After a week full of intense training, Mom and I headed back home. I was grateful I had the weekend to rest before Cowboy arrived at his forever home. It was a comfort knowing a trainer would come to my apartment every week to train with us and teach Cowboy to do other things that would be beneficial for me.

Quite a bit changed in my life after Cowboy and I began our partnership. The first few months were wonderful and exhausting, all at the same time, as we found our groove working together. But one lesson Cowboy taught me was completely unexpected: how to look beyond myself.

My sole focus for a number of years had been on me and readjusting to life. With Cowboy, I needed to be aware of his needs too—which helped me grow in more ways than I ever imagined. The more I learned to look past myself, the easier it became to relate to other people.

Cowboy also made me the most popular girl everywhere we went. That fear I once had about people staring at me because

I had a service dog came true. But what I hadn't considered was the *reason* people were staring. It wasn't because of my wheelchair—it was because of the handsome pup walking proudly beside me.

Not to mention, Cowboy was an incredible icebreaker. People would come right up to talk about my beautiful chocolate lab; more times than not, my wheelchair wasn't even a topic. I paused and smiled at the blessing I might have missed had I listened to the lies of my fear. I'm forever grateful I got out of my own way.

Chapter 11 - A Cowboy Comes to Town

To dig deeper into this chapter, turn to page 183 for Discussion Questions.

"But He said to me, "My grace is sufficient for you, for My power is made perfect in weakness." Therefore I will boast all the more gladly about my weaknesses, so that Christ's power may rest on me."
~ 2 Corinthians 12:9 (NIV)

CHAPTER TWELVE

A GOD CONNECTION

We had been living in the Lone Star State for four years when my stepdad's career moved our family once again, this time to the Pacific Northwest.

I missed Texans' Southern hospitality and their deep faith in God, but I enjoyed the beauty this part of the U.S. had to offer. After living in the South for so long, I had forgotten how much I loved the change of atmosphere that each new season brings.

As I settled into my new apartment, I surveyed the moving boxes all around me, most labeled KT's Kitchen or KT's Bedroom. I was proud of everything I had achieved so I could live independently, and I was incredibly appreciative for each opportunity I'd been given.

My mom had started a tradition on the first anniversary of my crash date. She didn't want that day to be one I mourned, but rather a day I was grateful for surviving. So every year on May 6, Mom and I would recall the blessings and lessons of that year.

While I didn't feel like I had accomplished much, once I looked at those boxes and realized how far I'd come since my injury, it inspired me to keep moving forward. I didn't want to become stagnant. I had gotten so much stronger physically, and I didn't want to stop there.

Eight years had passed since I graduated high school, and I finally felt mentally strong enough to put myself to the test. I decided to enroll in a class at a local community college. It was challenging and exhilarating at the same time—with the added bonus of proving wrong the trauma surgeon who predicted I would likely be in a vegetative state for the rest of my life. I earned an A in my first course. There was still something missing, though. I wanted what I had experienced in Texas: a God connection.

Living in the seated position has prompted me to lean on God more than ever. When I was first injured, I was full of anger and bitterness. It wasn't until I gave up my need for control that I realized God's plans for my life were far greater than anything I could have envisioned.

It's hard to grasp that the God who created the heavens and the earth is the same God who is in my corner, constantly answering my prayers. At first, I felt guilty about asking God for help with things such as transferring into bed. After all, He's God! Surely, He had more pressing matters on which to focus.

But I came to understand that I was putting limitations on a limitless God. The more I let go of the notion I was bothering Him with seemingly small tasks, the more I learned how He wanted me to come to Him with everything, regardless of its importance.

I still get stuck every now and then when I roll into bed, and I still ask God for help. It truly is amazing to feel that gentle nudge more times than not after I pray, allowing me to complete my transfer into bed.

I wanted to learn more about this God who was helping me through life, so the next semester I enrolled in a Christian university. Let me tell you, it was only by God's glorious grace I got into this school! My SAT and ACT scores were not up to par—but God obviously had a plan.

I signed up for two courses: New Testament history and literature, and a theology class. I quickly realized how little I knew about the Bible when I took my first baseline exam in the New Testament class. As I came to a question pertaining to the four gospels, I panicked. I didn't know anything about them, not even their names. I immediately felt unqualified for this class. After a few seconds of silently freaking out, I was overcome with peace, remembering the reason I was here—to learn more about God.

Someone once told me you should feel uncomfortable when you embark on a new season of life. It's when we are out of our comfort zones that we have the opportunity to grow. With that in mind, I embraced the not knowing and became excited about the learning.

One of my theology assignments was to speak with God for ten minutes a day in the privacy of my own home. The professor instructed our class to tell God everything about ourselves as if He didn't know anything. I thought that was a bit redundant because God is God, after all. He knows me better than I know myself!

But my professor brought up a good point that changed my way of thinking.

"God desires to have a personal relationship with each of us, and a relationship can't grow if only one contributes to it."

Those words were a huge eye-opener for me. I had been feeling God all around me—that was why I took this class. What I hadn't considered was God was with me whether I was learning about Him in a collegiate class or not. My grade wasn't going to bring me closer to God; that happened when

I intentionally set aside time to be with Him, to feel Him with me, and to let our relationship grow.

So, I went into my bedroom, parked my wheelchair at the foot of my bed, and set a timer on my phone for ten minutes. I had no idea what to say, so I began with a simple, *Hi, God.* I told Him all about myself, as if we were meeting for the first time. I felt a little strange at first, but eventually it started to feel natural.

After a week of this assignment, our professor gave us an update. He asked us to start talking with God about more personal subjects: our deepest wants, our hopes and dreams for the future, and even things that may be weighing on our hearts.

I took a deep breath, knowing this would be a heavy conversation. I sat in my bedroom and started talking with the Lord, telling him about my car crash and how much I wanted to be healed. I felt a tremendous sense of guilt as I spoke those words, and uncontrollable tears began streaming down my face.

As I exhaled a quivering breath, a warm, comforting sensation enveloped me. It was as if an unexplainable peace wrapped me in its arms as I continued to cry. I poured out my heart in those tears—every hurt, every disappointment, every regret—as this presence reassured me what I was feeling was okay.

My mind began trying to make sense of my emotions. *Why did I feel guilty about wanting to be healed?* I had craved that for so long, to be whole. And I knew this overwhelming blanket of peace was not in my head. It was authentic, and it was living in that moment with me.

I was desperate for some kind of clarity, so I reached for my phone and emailed my professor. It wasn't until after I sent the email that I felt this comforting presence return. This time, however, it not only wrapped me in peace but also offered me the answers I sought.

God showed me how I called on Him for help with each struggle I encountered. He prompted me to think of a typical day with me rolling down the sidewalk wearing a smile of gratitude. He revealed how He gives opportunities to people to help them rethink their situations. I smiled as I remembered experiencing a few of these instances. In that moment, I recalled times when people had come up to me saying the happiness that radiated from me, despite my circumstances, inspired them to be happy too.

I realized my guilt over asking God to heal me stemmed from my selfish desire to be"normal" again, to do things just like everyone else. I believe that guilt was my heart telling me I'm not meant to be normal. None of us are meant to be normal. We are meant to be extraordinary.

We achieve this through salvation (accepting Christ's offer of forgiveness for sin), by staying connected to God, by reading the Bible, and by trusting He has a perfect plan for each of us if we choose to partner with Him. Whether I'm healed or not, I want to continue living in God dependence! I went to bed that night with a sense of peace and gratitude in my heart.

I received a response from my professor the next morning.

"Consider the peace you felt as a gift," he wrote. "Sometimes things like that are not meant to be understood."

I had also written him about my paralysis.

"Only God knows why He allows healing to happen for some and not others. I will be praying for you, Katie."

He included a Bible verse that reaffirmed what the Lord had shown me the night before, and how I now viewed my broken body.

Three times I pleaded with the Lord to take it (ailment) away from me. But He said to me, "My grace is sufficient for you, for My power is made perfect in weakness." Therefore I will boast all the more gladly about my weaknesses, so that Christ's power may rest on me. That is why, for Christ's sake, I delight in weaknesses, in insults, in hardships, in persecutions, in difficulties. For when I am weak, then I am strong. (2 Corinthians 12:8-10 NIV)

I felt as if those words were written specifically for me. God was assuring me that my broken body truly is a blessing. His grace and His favor, that I in no way deserve, are sufficient because of my inadequacy. It is in my weaknesses I get to look beyond myself. They keep me tethered to God, relying on Him to guide me in ways that only He can do. My paralysis forces me to trust in something far greater than my limited abilities, giving me a chance at a full life in collaboration with God.

Even if I were free from the hardships of paralysis, I would still have other trials to overcome while standing on two feet. The Lord impressed upon my heart how He had always watched over me; but now that I was making an effort to know Him and talk with Him daily, I was living in relationship with Him.

The brokenness I once resented became the very brokenness for which I am now grateful. It reminds me in every moment of weakness how much I need God and His new mercies every day. I am not cursed because of my paralysis—I am blessed because of it.

That day, I smiled from a joy in my soul that has never left.

To dig deeper into this chapter, turn to page 186 for Discussion Questions.

"Always be joyful. Never stop praying. Be thankful in all circumstances, for this is God's will for you who belong to Christ Jesus."
~ 1 Thessalonians 5:16-18 (NLT)

CHAPTER THIRTEEN

BLESSINGS FROM BROKENNESS

A fork in the road.

That's how my mom described what I was facing several years earlier. She had pointed out that I could choose to stay depressed, wallowing in self-pity; or, I could choose to be thankful for the life I still have. She made me realize my mind and the thoughts I chose to let fill it were under no one else's control but my own.

I didn't see it then, but the miserable road of despair I was traveling was sucking the life out of me. Still, I wasn't sure I had enough energy to make the effort to be thankful.

But a truth emerged as I examined my life. Before my injury, I was living a life of entitlement. I thought I deserved a functioning body and much more just because I was a living, breathing human being. However, when I was stripped of that functioning body, I allowed myself to be blinded from seeing any good or hope in my life.

If I had a choice, would I be a quadriplegic confined to a wheelchair? No. Regardless, when I chose to look for the good in every situation, I created a new life of appreciation, not expectancy. In the beginning, it was a chore. Remember how I struggled when my mom challenged me to think of three things for which I was grateful? Looking back now, though, it was a chore that gave me life.

I didn't make this positive lifestyle choice to please others, but people seemed to take notice of my "attitude of gratitude." As I previously mentioned, strangers would come up and say I inspired them just by living my life with a genuine smile. These affirmations encouraged me to keep smiling, which led to other people smiling and finding contentment in their own lives. I'm pleased to be part of this beautiful cycle.

But despite experiencing more happiness in my life, it was a momentary emotion that relied heavily on my moods and what was happening around me. Occasionally, I would still get mentally and physically exhausted and think, *Why did God choose me for this life? I just want to be normal like everyone else!*

Living with paralysis in 75 percent of my body is much more complicated than not being able to move. All the other issues that come with immobility sometimes make it challenging to look on the bright side. For example, I have something called autonomic dysreflexia (AD), an overaction of my nervous system, which signals my body that something is uncomfortable below my level of injury.

So it's always a guessing game trying to discern the problem. Are my shoes too tight? Did I bruise my leg? Do I have a cramp in my calf? Or is this an indication that something more serious may be going on with my body? AD affects my blood pressure and heart rate; if ignored, it can lead to seizures and strokes.

Another constant issue is pressure sores. While they start out as small, red wounds or blisters, they can quickly become infected and spread; they can even lead to death. Periodically throughout the day, I must remember to shift my weight. If I forget, I can spend weeks in bed trying to heal from these sores.

Consequently, even after I improved my outlook, I still resented my body. Before God showed me my weakness has the power to make me stronger, I was more unstable than anyone knew. A few times a month, I would have breakdowns because I thought my life was unfair.

I used to believe these breakdowns were a normal part of life. Considering my situation, I reasoned that having them more frequently was just expected. I felt I was doing pretty good living the hand I had been dealt, yet I knew something was missing inside.

My family and friends, who loved and supported me every step of the way, couldn't fill this unexplainable void. I thought being accepted again by my peers would help me feel better. Being named Homecoming Queen and giving our graduation sendoff speech in high school had given me an incredible feeling, but it was momentary.

I was sure being able to do more for myself would help fill the hollowness. I worked my butt off in that rehab facility, and I'm proud of what I accomplished. But after getting myself into bed some nights, I would just lie there and weep. I asked God, *Why me?* more times than I can count.

When I shared about the crash at speaking engagements, I felt like I was doing something that could impact a life. Though it was uncomfortable to revisit that night over and over, the hope that my story could save others gave me purpose. But that still wasn't enough.

Even as much as I loved Cowboy—my loyal, four-legged helper—and as much as he guided me to grow in ways I didn't know I needed, he couldn't fill the emptiness either.

With each new endeavor, I was certain it would be the one to make me feel whole. That's a big reason why I had started college—to prove to myself that I could do it and fulfill a lifelong dream.

I confirmed I was bigger than my brain injury by acing my courses, yet I still didn't feel completely satisfied. At the same time, I began to realize something: I was looking in all the wrong places to feel whole. I thought if I could achieve the right accomplishment, status, relationship, or anything else the world could offer, it would complete me.

Instead, the void was finally filling up with God's love as I came to Him, vulnerable and raw, laying it all at His feet.

Until the theology assignment that led me to change how I viewed my brokenness, I had been frustrated with my body. But God showed me the wholeness I longed for wouldn't come from worldly things or even my physical healing. Only He could fill the God-shaped hole in my soul. I needed to focus on staying connected to my life source . . . God.

Just as my desire for eating food sustains my body, staying in fellowship with God sustains an even bigger part of who I am. The more I talk with God, read His Word, learn through Bible studies and sermons, live life with brothers and sisters in Christ as we encourage one another, and consciously invite Him into each day, the more I am made whole.

I used to interchange the words "happy" and "joy," thinking they had the same meaning. In fact, I preferred the word "happy" because somehow it felt better rolling off my tongue. But I now see the two words in very different lights. Today, I am filled with *joy*—the kind of joy the apostle Paul wrote about in Romans 15:13 (NIV): "May the God of hope fill you with all joy and peace as you trust in Him, so that you may overflow with hope by the power of the Holy Spirit."

This steadfast gift of joy differs greatly from the momentary happiness to which I once clung. It is a continuous way of life in connection with God that goes far beyond anything this world could offer. The Bible verse my professor sent me helped change my outlook on my injury—*His power is made perfect in my weakness.*

Instead of ruining my life, my broken body allows me to have true life in collaboration with God. Now, I'm not only grateful for the continual need for God my blessedly broken body demands, but also the smile I wear is not swayed by the ever-changing conditions of this world.

Joy is the byproduct of living in relationship with God. No matter what this world continues to throw at me, God is my strong foundation. Because of this, I can find joy in the most unfitting of circumstances.

Since my accident, I have been through several more challenges that, without leaning on God, could have wrecked me. Instead, they strengthen my faith, my awe of His steadfastness, and the joy in my soul. He continually proves He is close to me—all I have to do is look to Him and not to the temporary things before me.

I know that while this body of mine is weak, my soul is being strengthened day by day as long as my eyes are focused on eternal truth. Those monthly breakdowns of thinking, *Why me, Lord?* have turned into triumphant praises of, *Thank you, Lord, for choosing me for this life!*

Before my paralysis, I didn't fully appreciate God's miracles that abound each day, most of which I took for granted. However, when I look through the lens of God's abundant grace, my weakness truly has given me a new life.

We all are broken in some way, shape, or form. My physical brokenness just accentuated my spiritual brokenness and my need for Christ. None of us is worthy of His joy, grace, and forgiveness. Everlasting life is the amazing and transforming gift our Heavenly Father gives freely to all who earnestly come to Him, laying their sins at His feet.

I am blessed to live with Him in this joy and peace that surpasses understanding. His grace truly is sufficient.

To dig deeper into this chapter, turn to page 189 for Discussion Questions.

"For our light and momentary troubles are achieving for us an eternal glory that far outweighs them all. So we fix our eyes not on what is seen, but on what is unseen, since what is seen is temporary, but what is unseen is eternal." ~ 2 Corinthians 4:17-18 (NIV)

"The Lord is good, a refuge in times of trouble. He cares for those who trust in Him." ~ Nahum 1:7 (NIV)

"Yet I will rejoice in the Lord, I will be joyful in God my Savior." ~ Habakkuk 3:18 (NIV)

CHAPTER FOURTEEN

A BOOK, A CRASH, AND A CROSS

Everyone has some type of "car crash" to work through. It may be trying to regain a new normal in rehab, or it may be a parent of three trying to keep everyone alive and healthy. We decide whether our daily hurdles knock us down or propel us to soar over them on wings like eagles in alliance with God.

Letting go of situations that weigh us down and handing them to God can liberate and transform our lives. I'm speaking from experience because I am living my best life with a humble heart of gratitude—knowing the God of all creation is holding me despite whatever life throws my way.

Ten years, seven months, and twenty-five days after the crash that paralyzed me, my reliance on God would be put to the test once more.

My brother Jeff and I drove to Montana to spend Christmas with our dad. It was a wonderful two weeks enjoying a beautiful, snow-covered part of the country. During my stay, I noticed a barbed wire cross my stepmom had hanging on the wall.

"That's a really unique piece," I told her, admiring the cross. "I like it a lot!"

She told me a man in town makes them. And one just happened to show up in my stocking on Christmas morning!

We enjoyed Christmas Day with family and friends, filling our bellies with delicious food and enjoying each other's company.

"Have you ever thought of doing a daily devotional?" a friend inquired as we discussed my life.

"No, not really," I replied. "But I would love to do one eventually."

A few days later, she came by to give me a devotional she had bought for me. It's amazing how that book and the barbed-wire cross, which I believe were prompted by the Holy Spirit, would become so significant later on.

On the first day of the new year, my brother and I got up early so he could take me home, which was a two-day journey. A storm was headed our way, so we wanted to get on the road ahead of it. Our plan was to drive as far as we could the first day and stop at a hotel around 5:00 p.m. to watch the Green Bay Packers playoff game. The next day, we would finish the trip back to my apartment.

Jeff told me a few stories about Montana's history as we drove. We had made this trip together several times, and I always looked forward to spending time with him. We had been on the road for a couple of hours when suddenly, I heard my brother say, "Oh no. Oh no. NO!" I immediately looked up to see we were sliding on the icy road.

"Katie, hold on!" he yelled as he flung his arm across me, trying to protect me. Everything happened so fast. I remember watching my long hair as it fell straight up a few times. *That's weird,* I thought, but maintained a complete sense of peace. Moments later, the van stopped rolling and landed on its wheels.

Jeff and I were both dazed, not really comprehending what had just taken place. After sitting quietly for a few seconds, Jeff turned to look at me.

"How many times did we flip?" he asked.

"Maybe three or four times," I guessed as he slowly nodded.

Jeff abruptly snapped alert and immediately began looking me over for any obvious signs of injury. I told him I was okay, so he put his coat around me and got out to assess the damage. I still felt a little disoriented as I grappled to figure out what happened.

I looked up and noticed a lopsided, cross-shaped metal clip attached to my visor. "Bless This Car" was etched on it. I straightened it and thought, *Okay, we can go now.* Jeff returned to tell me the van was totaled. It wasn't until then I realized the windows and the windshield were all busted, and the car was filled with snow and chunks of earth. We weren't going anywhere!

All of a sudden, I remembered Cowboy had been in the vehicle with us. I swiftly checked to ensure he was okay. There he was, sitting very alert in the backseat, watching my brother inspect the car. I followed his gaze and noticed Jeff was only wearing a thin sweatshirt. I yelled for him to take his coat back.

"No! You will become hypothermic much quicker than I will."

A passing car pulled over to help. "Is there anything I can do for you guys?" the man asked.

"I can't find my cell phone," Jeff told him. "Would you call for an ambulance?"

As I watched my brother walk up to our good Samaritan, I realized what we had just survived. Despite a car rollover, I was uninjured and fully alert, as was Jeff. I shifted my focus to Cowboy, who was still sitting at attention. My heart was filled with an unexplainable joy I couldn't contain.

Another car stopped to help, and a gentleman—good Samaritan #2—immediately rushed over with a reflective emergency blanket that looked like a huge piece of tin foil. As Jeff thanked him and started wrapping it around my body, I began telling this stranger about God's mercy.

"I was in a car crash ten years ago that left me paralyzed. By the grace of God, we are all okay today!"

I was shaking uncontrollably, so Jeff asked the gentleman if he could put me in his car. Without hesitation, the man ran to his car to crank up the heat for me. My brother tried to open my door, but it was completely jammed shut. He went through the driver's side, carefully picked me up out of my wheelchair, and lifted me through his side of the van. He carried me to the warm car and got me settled.

Shortly afterward, more good Samaritans stopped, one in a car and another in a semitruck. One of them had an uncle in a wheelchair, so he had experience with these kinds of accessible vans. He explained to Jeff that my power wheelchair would be impounded with the vehicle if it wasn't removed. Thankfully, this man knew where the emergency unlock lever was to free my wheelchair from its lockdown system.

I watched as all those thoughtful men worked together to rip off the sliding side door to free my wheelchair. Jeff checked on me every few minutes to make sure I was still okay. I noticed his face and hands were chapped and bright red. I kept trying to coax him to sit in the car with me for a few minutes to warm up, but he refused, saying he needed to take care of things.

Cowboy was well taken care of too. Will, the truck driver, was kind enough to let my four- legged companion hang out in his truck and get warm. He also rescued my wheelchair and loaded it on the back of his truck. His last stop wasn't far from where Mom and Brian lived, so they met him a few days later to retrieve it.

When it was time to take me to the ambulance, I refused to let my brother transfer me. I knew he had to be sore from the accident, so Will graciously volunteered to carry me to the stretcher.

Jeff grabbed Cowboy, and they hopped in alongside me. An EMT (emergency medical technician) introduced herself as she cut off my coat, inspected my upper body, and wrapped a blood pressure cuff around my arm. I was still shaking uncontrollably, so she pulled out a quilt and tucked me into it like a burrito. It reminded me of how my mom used to do it when I was little.

My blood pressure was unstable, which indicated I was experiencing autonomic dysreflexia on the way to the hospital. And my body would not stop shaking. Even though my unsteady blood pressure was a cause for concern, I somehow knew I was going to be okay—we were all going to be okay. Jeff looked worried, so I kept reassuring him as the Holy Spirit filled me with peace.

Since I have no feeling below my chest, I was rushed in for scans as soon as we arrived at the hospital. They wanted to make sure I hadn't suffered any internal injuries. After the scans, I joyously told one of the emergency room nurses how good God is and how He had graciously saved my brother, my service dog, and me.

With a genuine smile, she responded, "You are the most joyous person I've ever had the pleasure of meeting in the ER!"

When I returned to the room where my brother and Cowboy were waiting, I noticed my furry friend had used his personality and good looks to charm the medical staff. Jeff was on the phone with our mom and dad, telling them what was going on. My heart ached for my brother as I listened to him explain the events of the past few hours. I could only imagine our parents' hysterical reaction.

I asked Jeff to hand me the phone so I could assure our mom we were completely fine, thanks to God's grace. The doctor came in and confirmed to her the only injuries we sustained were a few scrapes.

I was shocked to see Will walk into the ER a short while later. He had two objects in his hands and a look of disbelief on his face when he spotted me in the hospital bed with no serious injuries.

"I have never been much of a believer in God, but there is no way to logically explain what I'm seeing," he said, shaking his head.

He then showed me the devotional book my friend had given me, which had been tucked in my backpack before the crash. "The first thing I found in the wreckage was this book, lying face up. It was opened to this page."

Will began to read:

> *"Sometimes while driving, little annoyances can spur us into a prideful mindset: we are the only ones driving at a safe speed, or signaling correctly, or paying attention to the rules of the road. 'Why doesn't anyone else know what they are doing?!' The small things escalate quickly, and suddenly we're out of control, figuratively speaking.*
>
> *"It's pride, plain and simple. 'I have it all figured out and everyone else needs to get with it.' This kind of thinking is not only unpleasant for those around us, it's toxic to the soul. And it spreads quickly!*
>
> *"It's best to set the mind on Christ and his reconciliation . . . and set it quickly before we start condemning friends and family, too! In Christ, we're all just doing our best to get to where we need to go. We're not superior to anyone. We're not too terrible, either, because God created us and sent his son Jesus to die for us. This makes us worthy.*
>
> *"We are made right with God by placing our faith in Jesus Christ. And this is true for everyone who believes, no matter who we are. For everyone has sinned; we all fall short of God's glorious standard. (Romans 3:22-23, NLT)*

> *"Think on this today, whether you're on the road or not. Pray you'll arrive safely wherever you're going, and maybe try a pleasant wave to others on the way there."*[3]

Will had been driving behind Jeff and me when the accident occurred and shared with us what he had witnessed.

"I felt a strong gust of wind on my truck, and at the same time, I saw the back of your van being pushed by that same gust. That is when you lost control."

He kept praising my brother, saying Jeff had done all he could to get the van under control.

"I saw your car flip four times along the shoulder of the road."

Will began twisting his hands in circular motions to better describe how the van's back wheels became entangled with a barbed wire fence a few yards from the pavement.

"I'm amazed how the barbed-wire fence ultimately pulled you down and stopped the van from flipping into water nearby. But what astonished me most was when I spotted a barbed-wire cross in the middle of the road. I couldn't believe the irony."

---

[3]*A Little God Time for Women: 365 Daily Devotions.* Broadstreet Publishing Group LLC. August 2015, page 133. https://broadstreetpublishing.com/a-little-god-time-for-women-morning-and-evening-devotional/9781424560387

He handed me the cross and told me again how his belief in God became real after witnessing this miracle.

Another man, whom I didn't recognize, had joined us in my room. He smiled and came a few steps closer to me.

"Hi, Katie. I'm a pastor here in town, and your church notified me about your crash."

I was confused. I didn't understand how a pastor in Missoula, Montana, knew about our accident and had been sent by my hometown church. He saw I was perplexed and began to explain.

"My daughter is married to one of the pastors at your church. Your mom called the church to ask for prayers, so they reached out to me and asked if I would visit you at the hospital."

His presence was just another blessing on top of everything else I was feeling. I had so much joy and gratitude flowing through me, all I wanted to do was give thanks to God. So, with hearts overflowing, everyone in that room joined together to praise the Lord for sparing Jeff, Cowboy, and me that day.

I thought about the difference between my reaction that day as opposed to my first crash. Before, my eyes were fixed on the world and what I believed I had lost. I was too busy having a pity party to acknowledge that God was working amid my turmoil: the paramedics being in the right place at the right time, their quick action allowing me to breathe, the skilled physicians who worked on me, the caring staff at rehab, and all the friends, family, and strangers who prayed and stepped in to help. Most of all, God gifted my friend and me a second chance at life.

I am so blessed that God recast my vision to focus on Him. Witnessing His protective hand during the second accident gave me abundant joy that contradicted my circumstances. What had the potential to be overwhelming and frightening simply wasn't. Keeping my eyes on Him allowed me to feel His grace every moment.

The Lord weaves extraordinary events in and through our lives that are beyond our limited understanding. And He can use any experience to bring glory to Himself. I witnessed that firsthand in a Montana hospital the day God used a car crash, a devotional, and a barbed-wire cross to make a believer out of Will.

To dig deeper into this chapter, turn to page 191 for Discussion Questions.

"For we are God's handiwork, created in Christ Jesus to do good works, which God prepared in advance for us to do." ~ Ephesians 2:10 (NIV)

"Look to the Lord and His strength; seek His face always."
~ Psalm 105:4 (NIV)

"I lift up my eyes to the mountains—where does my help come from? My help comes from the Lord, the Maker of heaven and earth."
~ Psalm 121:1-2 (NIV)

CHAPTER FIFTEEN

ROLLING BY FAITH

Aren't you glad God doesn't hold grudges?

When my life was turned upside down, the last place I wanted to be was in the Lord's presence. While my bad decisions ultimately paralyzed me that night, God didn't hold that against me. Nor did His loving kindness diminish because I resented Him for my broken body. During this journey that led me to Jesus, I didn't realize that.

He worked—and is still working—on every part of what I thought destroyed my life, shaping it into something beautiful.

He taught me I have value because He made me in his own image.

He assured me there was nothing I could do or say that would cause Him to abandon me.

And He reminded me His body was broken too, when He hung on a cross and shed His blood for me.

After Jeff's and my accident, I decided not to go back to college. I could learn about God and strengthen my relationship with Him in other ways. He has surrounded me with an amazing church community and other believers who consistently strengthen my spiritual muscles. My home church is just as lively as those Texas churches that once overwhelmed me—but now I'm the one sitting in the front row, hands in the air, worshiping and praising Him with song.

I've learned that when we choose to rely on God in our times of trials, we have a unique opportunity to gain so much. This may sound easy, but it isn't. It requires us to let go of our desire for understanding and faithfully trust Him, even if it doesn't make sense. In 2 Corinthians 5:7, the apostle Paul tells believers to "walk by faith, not by sight."

God is the only one who can work all things together for good, but we have to give up the map we are clutching, trying to navigate our own way through life. In our hands, this map will deceive us. But if we let go of the control we think we have and allow God to take the helm, we will be amazed by His beautiful plans.

I can't stop smiling as I share this part of my story. When I gave my life to the Lord, I asked Him to work with whatever He could. One Sunday, as I was sitting in the front row at church, I lifted my hands up high in praise. When the service ended, a beautiful woman came up to me and asked if we could talk. She said she had come to church that morning carrying a heavy burden.

She shared how she felt her problem was an eight on a scale of ten. During worship, her eyes had been drawn to me. As she watched me swaying in my chair, smiling broadly as I sang, the weight of her problem seemed to diminish. By the end of the service, her problem no longer consumed her. As we continued our conversation, there was no denying the Holy Spirit had brought us together.

This beautiful soul's name is Christine Soule. She has a genuine heart for God and people. I was invigorated as she shared her story of triumph over trauma because of Jesus. But that wasn't the end of her story. Her passion for helping others, her commitment to saying "yes" to God's call, her diligence and hard work, along with other faith-filled believers, and the guidance of the Holy Spirit, were building blocks for creating a place of hope.

Christine founded Providence Heights, a Christ-centered entrepreneurial training center for women to discover their purpose while growing in their relationship with Jesus and each other.

I first met these women when I was invited to come share my story. As soon as I entered the doors, I felt the undeniable presence of the Holy Spirit. I fell in love with the women and the heart of Providence Heights. I knew I wanted to be involved when I learned of their mission: providing education and entrepreneurial training within a Christ-centered model. Plus, they believe a woman's circumstances do not define her.

A few months passed, and the stirring within my soul did not diminish. I finally asked Christine, "Is there any way I could be a part of Providence Heights?"

Unbeknownst to me, God was also placing me in Christine's heart during this time. They were looking for a life coach, but not just any life coach. Providence Heights was looking for a life coach with a heart for God, experience rising above trials, and a love for people.

"Have you ever considered becoming a life coach?" Christine responded.

I had no idea what a life coach was, but I wasn't going to let that stop me! I desired to be part of this incredible organization.

I came to Providence Heights for an interview and brought with me a résumé that wasn't impressive. Still, as I shared my story, it was evident my qualifications were more than what was listed on that piece of paper in front of them. It was God who brought me to Providence Heights, helped me through the life lessons to qualify me for this very position, and is still leading the way.

Today, I am a certified life coach, gratefully rolling alongside women in their journeys to never allow their own, God-given potential be paralyzed.

When I first began working at Providence, however, I didn't feel qualified. The enemy was whispering lies to me, telling me that I was unqualified because I lacked a college degree. But the team and women there helped me see that my life is my degree. God used all the difficult circumstances and painful lessons I've endured to prepare me for such a time as this.

I believe we all struggle with some form of paralysis in our lives. The devil's lies can be consuming without the truth of Jesus. I once thought my life had no value because of my brokenness. Now, I am blessed to help others see beyond theirs. Only God can take what the enemy meant for evil and make it good.

I correlate this part of my life to that of a precious gem. A pearl begins as something the oyster never wanted. But when a grain of sand irritates the oyster, it wraps the sand in multiple layers of protective coating, which over time is transformed into something beautiful.

When we choose to give God what is weighing on us, He wraps our weaknesses in His protective coating of grace. My paralysis was a huge frustration in my life, but it led me to God. The very irritant I wanted to be rid of was just the starting point for this pearl I now share with you.

God changes each of us from the inside out. Every time I ask for His help, talk with Him about my day, or just come to Him to rest, it's another chance for Him to wrap my weakness in His amazing grace. I have been transformed from someone who didn't even want a future . . . to being excited every day on this glorious journey. And it all started with a simple, *Hi, God.*

To dig deeper into this chapter, turn to page 193 for Discussion Questions.

A LETTER FOR YOU

Difficult circumstances are some of the best opportunities to see God at work in your own life. I pray my story will inspire you to give your weakness to God when the odds are stacked against you and you don't see any way ahead. I pray you will look up and choose to give thanks for the glimmers of God's goodness still around you.

I pray these gifts of gratitude will deepen your appreciation for your valuable life, and I pray you will choose to partner with God. His ways are sometimes confusing, but they are always good—better than anything we can comprehend. I can't wait to see the divine pearls you and the Lord create together.

Your life has value. Your life matters!

ABOUT THE AUTHOR

Katie Mathews began the journey of writing Unparalyzed more than twelve years ago. Her passion to help others live their own limitless journey with God was ignited when she changed her "attitude to gratitude" as she dealt with the aftermath of a horrendous car crash that left her a quadriplegic.

Her initial bitterness toward God dissipated as she realized He had always been with her, even during her darkest days. And, most importantly, He still had a plan for her life--despite her broken body.

Today, Katie is thriving in her career as a certified life coach for Providence Heights and Limitless Journey. Her desire is for all to break free from the paralysis of the mind and find freedom in partnership with God.

STAY CONNECTED

As God continues to accomplish amazing things in Katie's life, He has given her a heart for helping others. As a result, she has started a nonprofit called Limitless Journey.

Its calling is to empower people who are willing to find freedom through renewing their minds in partnership with God.

You can learn more about Limitless Journey at LimitlessJourney.org

Follow us on Facebook at facebook.com/ourlimitlessjourneys, and on Instagram, instagram.com/ourlimitlessjourneys.

We hope you'll join us in your Limitless Journey!

If you would like Katie to be a guest speaker at your event, please contact her at Katie@LimitlessJourney.org

DISCUSSION QUESTIONS

I believe we have all been shattered in one way or another. We live in a broken world, and we all make faulty decisions; but there is hope for a greater tomorrow. I'm grateful you decided to take this journey alongside me. I have been completely honest and transparent as I've shared my story.

I've learned that having a community, regardless of your stage in life, is vital. So, I've added questions about each chapter to let you know you're not alone in your struggles. I wish I could be with you, hear your answers to these questions, and sit with you as we discuss them. But I am praying for the Holy Spirit to be with you. Again, thank you for rolling alongside me with each flip of the page.

CHAPTER 1: A SHATTERED LIFE

"Be still and know that I am God!" ~ Psalm 46:10a (NLT)

LET'S DISCUSS:

We all have our own hypothetical car crashes in our lives. Something that leaves us shattered in pieces on the floor.

How have you experienced times in your life that shattered you?

Whether you're in that season right now, you're walking with someone who is, or you have been through one, I pray you will be uplifted in your brokenness to become whole again.

PRAYER:

Lord, help keep us together when we feel we are in pieces . . . nothing but shattered glass on the floor. Please help us to trust You when we don't understand. Help us to remember You are good, and You are in control, even when we don't believe our circumstances reflect that.

CHAPTER 2: A GRIM PROGNOSIS

"The Lord is close to the brokenhearted and saves those who are crushed in spirit." ~ Psalm 34:18 (NIV)

LET'S DISCUSS:

Fifteen years after the car accident with Chelsea, I received a Facebook message from the daughter of the paramedic who was first at the crash scene. His daughter told me they had been praying for me ever since the accident. She then set up a meeting for Jon and me to talk on Christmas Eve.

I was finally able to thank him for saving me. We were both in tears as we talked about that day. Jon told me he had been a paramedic for over fifteen years when my crash happened. He said he can sense whether someone will make it or not. As he lifted me into the helicopter, he doubted that I would live. He prayed for Chelsea and me at that moment, then called the local Christian radio station and asked listeners to pray for us too.

Jon's hunch about me wasn't far off base. During my initial days in the trauma center, doctors and surgeons worked tirelessly trying to keep me alive. My family had plenty of reason to lose hope as they received devastating news about my condition.

Think about a time when you've had reason to lose hope. How did/do you keep moving?

Even though my prognosis did not look good, the trauma surgeon faithfully came each day to meticulously clean out my lungs.

Have you had someone in your life—or been that someone—who is like this trauma surgeon?

Maybe you've been the one to pray for someone over and over again, even though the situation seemed hopeless. Or maybe you've been the one being prayed over.

What does it feel like being the one giving/receiving this life-sustaining help?

PRAYER:
Lord, even when there seems to be no hope, please give us strength.

CHAPTER 3: THE MISSING YEARS

"For I know the plans I have for you,' declares the Lord, 'plans to prosper you and not to harm you, plans to give you hope and a future."~ Jeremiah 29:11 (NIV)

LET'S DISCUSS:

My brain injury caused severe, short-term memory loss, and I reverted back to believing I was a thirteen-year-old girl. I felt frustrated because no one understood what I was going through. My confusion, my broken body, and my extreme discomfort made me feel alone and overwhelmed.

Do you ever feel like the odds are stacked against you? Or that you are completely out of control? Have you been confused as to why God allows something to happen?

Even when we don't understand, God is still working on our behalf.

PRAYER:

Lord, please help us to know that Your ways are good. The things that happen to us and the things in this world are not always good, but You are! Please help us remember this truth when we don't understand. Please help us hold tight to the truth that You are always with us. You are still in control.

CHAPTER 4: A NEW NORMAL

"Finally, brothers and sisters, whatever is true, whatever is noble, whatever is right, whatever is pure, whatever is lovely, whatever is admirable—if anything is excellent or praiseworthy—think about such things." ~ Philippians 4:8 (NIV)

LET'S DISCUSS:

When I finally left rehab and returned home, I talked about having everything I needed: a loving support system, a home and vehicle fitted to my needs, and wonderful caregivers. Yet, I let paralyzing thoughts fill my head instead of counting my blessings.

Think of a time when your thoughts were focused on the negative more than the positive.

How was that for you?

What effects did it have in your life?

If you're still in that space, how are you willing to change your thoughts to change your life?

You do have power within you to renew your mind and renew your life!

PRAYER:

Thank You, Lord, for giving us the ability to choose the way we want to live. Please help us be mindful whether our thoughts are holding us captive or setting us free. I pray that we partner with You and choose a positive, joy-filled life.

CHAPTER 5: WHAT'S NEXT?

"Don't worry about anything; instead, pray about everything. Tell God what you need, and thank Him for all He has done. Then you will experience God's peace, which exceeds anything we can understand. His peace will guard your hearts and minds as you live in Christ Jesus."
~ Philippians 4:6-7 (NLT)

LET'S DISCUSS:

I was so focused on pleading with God for an answer as to why He let me become paralyzed, it never occurred to me I still had things for which to be grateful. I couldn't see beyond feeling betrayed by an all-powerful God. But my mom helped me realize if I changed my attitude to one of gratitude, my outlook would change . . . and she was right.

Is there something in your life you need to reexamine and view through the lens of gratitude?

"Look after each other so that none of you fails to receive the grace of God. Watch out that no poisonous root of bitterness grows up to trouble you, corrupting many."
~ Hebrews 12:15 (NLT)

It is scientifically proven that gratitude and anxiety cannot exist in the brain at the same time. It's your choice!

Are you willing to walk/roll with me and intentionally find three things to be grateful for each day?

Let's start today!

1.
2.
3.

PRAYER:

Lord, thank You for giving us minds that are powerful! I ask You to illuminate your beautiful gifts around us and help us to be grateful. Please give us strength in the days we aren't appreciative, and help us to renew our minds so our lives can be renewed.

CHAPTER 6: GOD SENDS A UNICORN

"My thoughts are nothing like your thoughts, says the Lord. And My ways are far beyond anything you could imagine. For just as the heavens are higher than the earth, so My ways are higher than your ways and My thoughts higher than your thoughts." ~ Isaiah 55:8-9 (NLT)

LET'S DISCUSS:

Meeting Donna was like meeting a unicorn. A quadriplegic who is independent was supposed to be impossible! God restored my hope for a brighter future in the form of a fearless woman sitting next to me.

In what ways have you experienced unexpected hope?

PRAYER:

Thank you, Lord, that Your ways are far greater than our ways! I am so grateful You see beyond our limited viewpoint, and that You have good plans to lead us to the finish line safely—even if it's not the way we planned. Please, help us look up and trust You with our journeys.

CHAPTER 7: BUDDING INDEPENDENCE

"All hard work brings a profit, but mere talk leads only to poverty." ~ Proverbs 14:23 (NIV)

"Do not conform to the pattern of this world, but be transformed by the renewing of your mind. Then you will be able to test and approve what God's will is—His good, pleasing, and perfect will." ~ Romans 12:2 (NIV)

LET'S DISCUSS:

I encourage you to start examining your thoughts. Are they typically geared toward "I can't" with a number of valid explanations?

Because of all the seemingly reasonable limitations put on me, I didn't have much hope for my future.

What limitations are you holding onto? Do they exist because someone placed them on you? Are they due to your circumstances? Or maybe they're the result of your own self-doubt?

Let's visualize together. Gather up all your limitations, including your own thoughts about what can and can't be done. Now, let's lay them down at the foot of the cross.

Jim had me imagine the things I wanted to do for myself without any preconceived limitations. I encourage you to invite Jesus into your space and ask Him to show you what it would look like to live limitlessly with Him. Write it down.

In the words of Jim: “There are so many different ways to do the same thing, you just have to figure out your way. It doesn’t matter how awkward or silly you look doing it, as long as you can get it done, that’s your way.”

Are you willing to keep taking steps forward when things, once again, seem impossible?

PRAYER:
Lord, we are limitless with You. Please give us the strength and stamina to battle through these lessons in life that make us prepared for what lies ahead. Help us open our minds to what we can accomplish with You.

CHAPTER 8: HEALING THROUGH THE PAIN

"Do not be overcome by evil, but overcome evil with good." ~ Romans 12:21 (NKJV)

"And we know that in all things God works for the good of those who love Him, who have been called according to His purpose." ~ Romans 8:28 (NIV)

LET'S DISCUSS:

What life-shattering events have you been through?

When I first started sharing my story about the dangers of distracted driving, I was ashamed. Getting in front of an audience and sharing my bad decisions wasn't something I would willingly see myself doing. What's amazing, though, is every time I shared my testimony, I took one more step toward healing. Plus, I knew I had the potential to help at least one person who was listening. The very part of my life that I once wished I could delete had become my purpose.

There is power in our testimonies—that's why the enemy wants to silence us!

I encourage you to look at your brokenness in a different light.

Where have you seen God's hand in your story?

Did you and/or others learn valuable lessons from this time?

What blessings, no matter how small, have come forth from it?

The world needs your testimony!

PRAYER:
Lord, thank You that You are the One who takes what the enemy meant for evil and uses it for good. I pray for us to continually give You our brokenness and the things we don't understand and trust You to guide us through the mess. Help us to help one another through the power of our testimonies!

CHAPTER 9: SPREADING MY WINGS

"But those who wait on the Lord shall renew their strength; they shall mount up with wings like eagles, they shall run and not be weary, they shall walk and not faint."
~ Isaiah 40:31 (NKJV)

"Our help is in the name of the Lord, the Maker of heaven and earth." ~ Psalm 124:8 (NIV)

LET'S DISCUSS:

Living independently left me no choice but to ask for God's help on many occasions. Looking back now, I see that He was, and still is, my helper.

Here are some of the descriptive names of God from the Bible:

- Jehovah Ezer: The Lord Our Helper
- El Shaddai: Lord God Almighty
- El Channun: Gracious God
- El Rio: The God Who Sees Me
- Jehovah-Raah: The Lord My Shepherd
- Jehovah Rapha: The Lord That Heals
- Jehovah Jireh: The Lord Will Provide
- Jehovah Shammah: The Lord Is There
- Jehovah Tsidkenu: The Lord Our Righteousness
- Jehovah Mekoddishkem: The Lord Who Sanctifies You
- Jehovah Metshodhathi: The Lord My Fortress
- Jehovah Shalom: The Lord Is Peace[4]

Where do you see these characteristics of God ringing true in your life?

PRAYER:

Lord, You are good. Help us to see Your good attributes within our lives and to know You are near at all times.

[4]"The Names of God in the Old Testament," Blue Letter Bible, Study Resources. https://www.blueletterbible.org/study/misc/name_god.cfm

CHAPTER 10: THIS AIN'T MY FIRST RODEO

"O God, we meditate on your unfailing love."
~ Psalm 48:9a (NLT)

LET'S DISCUSS:

Sometimes we benefit from having wonderful people in our lives because of a situation we'd rather not have gone through. Has this been true in your life?

"Impossible" is now a word that stimulates me. Often, I've found that people misuse this word because they can't comprehend how something can be done. With God all things are possible! If it is His will for you to do something, by golly, you will if you partner with Him! Here are some scriptures that have spoken to me in this area.

Romans 12:2 (NIV): "Do not conform to the pattern of this world, but be transformed by the renewing of your mind. Then you will be able to test and approve what God's will is—His good, pleasing, and perfect will."

Ephesians 2:8-10 (NIV): "For it is by grace you have been saved, through faith—and this is not from yourselves, it is the gift of God—not by works, so that no one can boast. For we are God's handiwork, created in Christ Jesus to do good works, which God prepared in advance for us to do."

Ephesians 3:20-21 (NIV): "Now to Him who is able to do immeasurably more than all we ask or imagine, according to

His power that is at work within us, to Him be glory in the church and in Christ Jesus throughout all generations, for ever and ever! Amen."

Can you see the thread here? If we don't conform/listen to the lies of the world but instead listen to the truth of God and seek to become whom He has created us to be, we are limitless. We are limitless because it is His power working within us. But people will doubt because they haven't yet seen our partnership with God.

PRAYER:

Lord, help us fix our eyes on You, so we may become the people You created us to be. You have given each of us gifts and talents that are unique and wonderful! You knit us together in our mother's womb, and You have a plan for each of us. Please, help us to step forward in faith and break past all our impossibles!

CHAPTER 11: A COWBOY COMES TO TOWN

"But be sure to fear the Lord and faithfully serve Him. Think of all the wonderful things He has done for you." ~ 1 Samuel 12:24 (NLT)

LET'S DISCUSS:

Initially, I did not want a service dog because I thought it would draw attention to the fact I was in a wheelchair. However, when I did get more attention, it wasn't because of the wheelchair—it was because of my handsome pup.

What things have you expected to be a certain way, but were pleasantly surprised when they weren't?

I have been writing this book for several years, and Cowboy has since passed away. His death was unexpected and more heartbreaking than I can express. I stayed at my mom's house to grieve. I did not want to get another service dog—I wasn't going to let anything replace my love for Cowboy.

My mom has three dogs, and they were all a comfort to me as I mourned. I stayed with Brian and my mom for a few weeks; Mom secretly called Service Dogs, Inc. while I was there. The night before I went home, Mom sat in bed with me with all three of her dogs.

"Did being here with these guys help you?" she asked as she ruffled the fur atop the retriever's head.

I looked at her, not knowing where she was going with this, but nodded my head. I couldn't help but smile as Bella leaned into my mom's hand, enjoying the head scratch.

"You know they're not Cowboy, right?" she continued.

I gave her a confused and slightly insulted look.

She smiled, saying, "If you get another service dog, it's not going to replace Cowboy. The new dog will have his or her own personality, just like my dogs."

I gave her a smirk and sighed. She was right.

"Sweetie, would you be willing to look into getting another service dog?"

I took a deep breath, knowing how long it took me to get Cowboy, and let my spirit say yes as I nodded.

"Good!" my mom exclaimed. "I already called Service Dogs, Inc., and they have the perfect dog for you. He was trained for a woman in a wheelchair who backed out at the last moment, and he's just been waiting for his person."

Templeton did not replace Cowboy in my life; my love for my first faithful companion will never die. But Templeton is another immense blessing. As I type this, I look through grateful tears at him curled up on the couch. Sometimes, heartbreak can lead to beautiful blessings.

Are you open to all God has for you following heartache?

PRAYER:
Lord, thank You for beautiful blessings we don't know we need. I pray for us to be open to all You have for us.

CHAPTER 12: A GOD CONNECTION

"But He said to me, "My grace is sufficient for you, for My power is made perfect in weakness." Therefore I will boast all the more gladly about my weaknesses, so that Christ's power may rest on me." ~ 2 Corinthians 12:9 (NIV)

LET'S DISCUSS:

My mom helped me see each anniversary of my crash date as an opportunity to review the previous year and be grateful for all I had accomplished.

What circumstances within your life can you reframe?

"A relationship can't grow if only one is contributing to it," my theology professor told me.

God's biggest desire is for us to have a personal relationship with Him and partner with Him in our daily lives. The Bible says that when we draw near to God, He draws near to us.

Are you willing to grow closer to God?

I mentioned not wanting to bother God by asking for something I considered small in the grand scheme of things.

In what ways have you been unwilling to bring your circumstances to God?

I believe the key to hearing God is having an open heart and looking for the different and often subtle ways He communicates.

Sensing how God is communicating with us can happen in so many ways.

What are some ways you feel the Lord is communicating with you?

How has He done so in the past?

I most often sense God by feeling tickles on my cheek or my chin. I know that may sound strange, but it's a way that He and I communicate.

The verse that changed how I viewed my circumstances was 2 Corinthians 12:9. Let's look at that verse in conjunction with the following verse:

"But He said to me, 'My grace is sufficient for you, for My power is made perfect in weakness.' Therefore I will boast all the more gladly about my weaknesses, so that Christ's power may rest on me. That is why, for Christ's sake, I delight in weaknesses, in insults, in hardships, in persecutions, in difficulties. For when I am weak, then I am strong." 2 Corinthians 12:9-10 (NIV)

"For when I am weak, then I am strong" sounds backward, doesn't it? I can say from personal experience this is true. When we take our weaknesses to the Lord and let Him fill us, we become more than we ever could on our own.

In what ways are you willing to partner with God within your weaknesses?

PRAYER:

Lord, it sounds so strange to say that when we are weak, we are strong. Thank You that this is true when we come to You. Thank You for wanting us to live with You and for filling us with what we need. I pray that we will continue to draw near to You all the days of our lives. Please open our eyes and hearts so we may sense Your presence.

CHAPTER 13: BLESSINGS FROM BROKENNESS

"Always be joyful. Never stop praying. Be thankful in all circumstances, for this is God's will for you who belong to Christ Jesus." ~ 1 Thessalonians 5:16-18 (NLT)

LET'S DISCUSS:

The Bible says we have the mind of Christ (1 Corinthians 2:16). However, we often allow thoughts, doubts, fears, and waywardness to creep into our lives when we listen to the devil's lies. But we can uproot those weeds and replace them with truth and renew our lives! The verse that gives me the confidence and power to continually renew my life is Romans 12:2. (Romans 12:1-2 are my favorite verses!)

Romans 12:2 (NIV): "Do not conform to the pattern of this world, but be transformed by the renewing of your mind. Then you will be able to test and approve what God's will is—His good, pleasing, and perfect will."

In Philippians 4:8, the apostle Paul gives us a roadmap for renewing and staying on track with our thoughts.

Philippians 4:8 (NIV): "Finally, brothers and sisters, whatever is true, whatever is noble, whatever is right, whatever is pure, whatever is lovely, whatever is admirable—if anything is excellent or praiseworthy—think about such things."

In what ways can renewing your mind impact your life? What would it look like if you laid down your expectations

for how things should be and instead gave a sacrifice of gratitude?

I talked about finding three things to be grateful for each day, no matter how tired I felt.

What disciplines will you put into place to help you thrive as you renew your mind?

We are eternal beings inside temporary bodies. I talked about a God-shaped hole I was continually trying to fill with worldly things. I'm not saying accomplishments are bad, but we need a balance in our lives.

In what ways are you permitting the Lord to fill that God-shaped hole within you each day?

PRAYER:
Lord, things in our lives and in the world are often not good and can cloud our minds. But, God, You are always good. We lay our own expectations at Your feet and take up Your good, pleasing, and perfect will. Please help us renew our minds and clear our vision to see Your beautiful blessings all around us.

CHAPTER 14: A BOOK, A CRASH, AND A CROSS

"For our light and momentary troubles are achieving for us an eternal glory that far outweighs them all. So we fix our eyes not on what is seen, but on what is unseen, since what is seen is temporary, but what is unseen is eternal." ~ 2 Corinthians 4:17-18 (NIV)

"The Lord is good, a refuge in times of trouble. He cares for those who trust in Him." ~ Nahum 1:7 (NIV)

"Yet I will rejoice in the Lord, I will be joyful in God my Savior." ~ Habakkuk 3:18 (NIV)

LET'S DISCUSS:

In what ways have you seen God work in the "car crashes" of your own life?

What is the posture of your heart in the times you lack understanding?

Will's last stop on his truck route happened to be close to the city where I lived. After I was released by the hospital in Montana and got back home, I went to the emergency room to get a few more things checked out. Will showed up at the ER clutching two items in his hands—one was a gift for me and the other one was for him.

He handed me a silver cross keychain and kept an identical one. We both now have the crosses on our key rings.

"This will be a reminder for me to never forget God's mercy and what I experienced," he explained.

God may allow things to happen in our lives for the good of others. When our eyes are fixed on the Lord more than the circumstances, it's a beautiful thing.

In what ways can you thank God for moments you once wished hadn't happened?

If you are willing, I encourage you to talk with God about this.

My relationship with the Lord, even though it was just beginning, gave me a peace that surpassed understanding during this time. If you haven't already, I encourage you to invite God into your life by talking with Him and reading His Word (the Bible). An easy way to start today is by downloading the Bible app on your phone. He wants to be active in each of our lives.

PRAYER:

Father, thank You for saving us day after day. Thank You for fighting on our behalf in ways we don't even see. We know Your ways are far greater than our ways. Please open our hearts and our hands to give You the circumstances we don't understand. Please open our eyes to see Your blessings all around us.

CHAPTER 15: ROLLING BY FAITH

"For we are God's handiwork, created in Christ Jesus to do good works, which God prepared in advance for us to do."
~ Ephesians 2:10 (NIV)

"Look to the Lord and His strength; seek His face always."
~ Psalm 105:4 (NIV)

"I lift up my eyes to the mountains—where does my help come from? My help comes from the Lord, the Maker of heaven and earth." ~ Psalm 121:1-2 (NIV)

LET'S DISCUSS:

I am so thankful the God of the universe doesn't hold grudges. I gave Him plenty of reasons when I blamed Him for feeling hopeless and worthless, when I resented Him for my broken body, and when I refused to acknowledge that He was right beside me, loving me through it all.

It was these circumstances that led me to Jesus. What I thought destroyed my life, He shaped into something beautiful.

There's a freedom that comes when we step out in faith and hand the reins to the Lord. It means we are willing to take that leap because of the trust we have in God. We no longer need to carry burdens like worry or guilt; God is in control of even the tiniest details of our lives.

I love the definition of faith a friend shared with me: When we walk to the edge of all the light we have and take that step into the darkness of the unknown, we must believe that one of two things will happen. There will be something solid for us to stand on . . . or God will teach us to fly.

Think of a time when it was especially difficult for you to step out in faith and trust God. What was the outcome?

God wants to partner with you in your life.

Are you ready to take His hand and see the fulfilling things He has planned for you?

If you've never experienced freedom in Christ, I urge you to make that commitment today. How?

- Acknowledge that you're a sinner
- Confess your sins to God
- Ask Him to forgive you of your sins
- Invite Jesus into your heart
- Accept Him as Lord and Savior of your life

PRAYER:
Jesus, give each of us a willing heart and the courage to step out in faith like never before. Fill us with a faith that can move mountains. Help us realize that sometimes we must endure affliction so we can grow and provide comfort and encouragement to others. Thank You for blessing us. Please, help us to not let obstacles become larger than our faith.

If you enjoyed this book, I'd be so grateful if you'd **WRITE A REVIEW....**

It's easy and helps my book get into the hands of more readers.

- Step 1: Go To www.AMAZON.com
- Step 2: Search for my book in Amazon books
- Step 3: Scroll down to REVIEWS
- Step 4: Leave a Review

I'd love to know your thoughts about my book. Contact me at Katie@limitlessjourney.org & let me know what you got out of the book.

Join my newsletter for more info on events and releases.

Sign up here: www.limitlessjourney.org.

Thank You for Your Support.

Katie Mathews

Founder of Limitless Journey
Life Coach | Author | Speaker

"Life is not about what happens to you. It's about how you choose to respond."

Katie's passion is for all to take hold of their own unlimited potential. Join her on a transformative journey where she will empower you to discover freedom through renewing your mind in partnership with our Creator. Drawing from her own remarkable journey from a shattered existence to a life of value and purpose, she offers a compelling narrative that aims to invigorate you to rise above your limitations. You'll explore actionable steps that will empower you to transform your future.

What's holding you back from thriving within your own Limitless Journey?

Topics:

- Discover power within weakness
- The transforming benefits of gratitude
- Choosing to renew the mind
- Stepping into partnership with our Creator
- Living a fulfilled life of value

Great For:

- Keynote
- Church Services
- Conferences

Book To Speak:

Katie@LimitlessJourney.org | www.limitlessjourney.org

At Square Tree Publishing, we believe your message matters. That is why our dedicated team of professionals is committed to bringing your literary texts and targeted curriculum to a global marketplace. We strive to make that message of the highest quality, while still maintaining your voice.

We believe in you, therefore, we provide a platform through website design, blogs, and social media campaigns to showcase your unique message. Our innovative team offers a full range of services from editing to graphic design inspired with an eye for excellence, so that your message is clearly and distinctly heard.

Whether you are a new writer needing guidance with each step of the process, or a seasoned writer, we will propel you to the next level of your development.

At Square Tree Publishing, it's all about launching YOU!

Apply TODAY to become a Square Tree author.
Go to www.squaretreepublishing.com
Click the **APPLY NOW** button.

Made in the USA
Columbia, SC
27 September 2024